pony
handbook

DAVID TAYLOR
BVMS, FRCVS, FZS

David Taylor is a well-known veterinarian and broadcaster and the author of over 30 books, including six volumes of autobiography, some of which formed the basis for three series of the BBC television drama *One by One*.

He has also written *Barron's Small Pet Handbook* and *Collins Family Pet Guides: Rabbit*. The founder of the International Zoo Veterinary Group, he has exotic patients around the world, ranging from crocodiles to killer whales and giant pandas. He lives in Surrey, England, with his wife and five cats.

pony
handbook

David Taylor
BVMS, FRCVS, FZS

First edition for the United States, its territories, possessions, and dependencies, Canada, and the Philippine Republic published by Barron's Educational Series, Inc., 2002.

Originally published in English by HarperCollins*Publishers* Ltd under the title: COLLINS PONY HANDBOOK

All inquiries should be addressed to:
Barron's Educational Series, Inc.
250 Wireless Boulevard
Hauppauge, New York 11788
http://www.barronseduc.com

International Standard Book No. 0-7641-5426-5

Library of Congress Catalog Card No. 2001087184

This book was created by
SP Creative Design
Editor: Heather Thomas
Art Director and Production: Rolando Ugolini
Photography: Rolando Ugolini
Additional Photography: Kit Houghton: pages 14 and 18–29

Color reproduction by Colourscan, Singapore
Printed and bound by Printing Express Ltd, Hong Kong

9 8 7 6 5 4 3 2 1

CONTENTS

INTRODUCTION

Almost every one of the multitude of people across the world who takes to the saddle every year began his or her special relationship with *Equus* by way of one of the smallest representations of the horse family, the pony. The jockeys in the Belmont Stakes or the Grand National, the outback farmer doing the rounds of his stock, the mounted policeman—all these, and millions more—in most cases started riding on a little, often impish, sometimes downright willful pony.

In Britain and elsewhere in the Western world, ponies and pony riding are increasing steadily in popularity. Pony clubs thrive in the suburbs, city centers, and the countryside; pony trekking vacations attract ever more enthusiasts; and each day as I drive around in a car, the number of cheerful youngsters mounted on rascally Thelwell look-alikes seems to increase. Although ponies are often used to pull, carry, and otherwise transport people and things, they are far more complex and wonderful than that. They are more than pets, more than a hobby or a pastime, more than mere beasts of burden. Ponies are philosophers and companions, confidants, and friends. Ponies are magic.

This book is for the amateur, the dabbler, the beginner, and all those lucky individuals who are falling firmly under the spell of the most superior of domesticated animals.

CHAPTER ONE
EVOLUTION AND BREEDS

Ponies developed over the eons in ways that were quite different from those of other groups of herbivores. Their bodies adapted to digest the cellulose-containing plant material that was now abundant on the dry land of the earth. And to protect themselves from dangerous, non-herbivorous predators, the biological process of natural selection produced their characteristic speed and nimbleness, their sharp reactions and highly tuned senses. Only much later, when humans arrived upon the scene and recognized their potential for domestication, did artificial selection—the breeding of equines to create types for specialized forms of work—begin.

EVOLUTION OF THE PONY

About 55 million years ago, in what are now called Europe and North America but that were then joined together in one landmass, a little doglike animal moved through the forests, grazing on low shrubs. This was *Hyracotherium*, ancestor of the horse and also of the rhinoceros and tapir. Descended itself from forebears possessing the basic five toes per foot, it had already lost two outer toes on its hindfeet and one inner toe on its forefeet, the remaining toes looking doglike, with pads; there was no sign of hooves as yet. It had a short muzzle and a long tail curved like a cat's.

As the eons passed, the descendants of *Hyracotherium* split off into numerous branches of the family tree. The rhinos and tapirs went their way; the equine branch went theirs, discarding more toes so that they might concentrate on the perfection of a single, highly modified toe on each foot, growing larger, developing teeth that were ideal for cropping and grinding grass, and acquiring large, efficient eyes.

By about one million years ago, all the surviving equine descendants of the original *Hyracotherium* had settled into four main groups: the horses, the asses, the half-asses, and the zebras. They were distributed (as shown in the diagram) in fairly specific parts of Africa, Europe, and the Middle East, with almost no overlapping of the various groups. The zebras were purely southern African and the half-asses (ancestors of the onager, kulan, kiang, and djiggetai, and of the hemione that became extinct about a hundred years ago) were all Asiatic. The asses, from which donkeys were developed, were purely northern African, and the horses (including ponies, which are simply horses under 14.2 hands high) were inhabitants of Europe and of western Asia.

By the Ice Age, scientists could identify four major types of horse or pony existing in the world and, with the disappearance of all horses in the Americas by about 6000 B.C.E. (being reintroduced much later by the Spanish conquistadors), this means solely in Europe and western Asia. The cause of the horse's demise in the Americas is the subject of much speculation. Changes in climate or food availability were probably not involved, for other large herbivores, such as the bison, survived and prospered. Some scientists believe that a virulent viral or protozoal disease, probably carried by insects, may have swept across the continent killing the equines, but the reason remains one of the great unsolved mysteries.

EQUINE DISTRIBUTION OVER THE LAST ONE MILLION YEARS

Continents originally joined here

Horses

Horses

Half-asses

Asses

Zebras

THE FOUR TYPES OF PONY

From the four types, our modern horse and pony breeds are descended.

▲ **Type 1** was a pony of northwestern Europe, standing about 12.2 hands and in many respects very similar to the Exmoor ponies of today.

▲ **Type 2** was also a pony but heavier than type 1. Its height was up to 14.2 hands and its coat was lighter colored. Most of the European horses of the early Stone Age seem to have been of this type. It most closely resembled the Przewalski horse of today.

▲ **Type 3** was a central Asian horse of around 15 hands. This long-headed equine did not apparently play a significant part in later horse and pony evolution.

▲ **Type 4** was strictly a pony, although it is often referred to as a fine-boned small horse. It grew up to 12 hands and lived in western Asia. The modern pony that most closely resembles it is the Caspian pony from Iran.

Modern ponies are generally thought to be made up from crossings between some or all of the four types. Crosses between types 1 and 4 probably led to the tarpan, a wild horse that survived in Russia, eastern Europe, and Germany until the nineteenth century. (By selecting breeds that possibly most closely resemble the tarpan, such as Icelandic ponies and Gotland horses, crossing them through several generations, it has been possible to "recreate" the extinct animal in recent years.) The tarpan is an ancestor of many pony breeds that we know today, including the Konik of Poland, the Bosnian pony of Yugoslavia, the Hucul of the Carpathian mountains, and the Scweike of Poland.

BELOW: *Our modern pony breeds have all evolved from the earliest types of pony. They come in a variety of different sizes, coat types, and colors.*

DOMESTICATION

This began around 3000 B.C.E., almost certainly in eastern Europe (the Ukrainian and Russian steppes), Kazakhstan, and in the steppes of western Asia, mainly around Lake Aral. From these areas, the domestic equine spread outward after 2000 B.C.E., although the Sumerians had also been domesticating onagers as early as 3000 B.C.E. in what is now Iraq. Type 2 was the first to be domesticated for riding and pack work, probably by reindeer herdsmen. Following that, types 4 and then 3 were broken for harnessing to chariots. Finally, type 1 was tamed, originally to be used as a pack animal since asses and mules were unknown to Europeans north of the Alps before about 100 C.E. Before 600 B.C.E., all the "horses" ridden or driven by ancient civilizations were in fact ponies!

All "wild" ponies (excluding the Przewalski horse), which exist today and including the nine British breeds (see pages 18–23), should really be called "feral," descendants of the domesticated stock that went back to the wild. The brumbies of Australia, many of which are annually trapped, slaughtered, and processed for pet food, are descended from domestic ponies imported by the settlers and have been breeding in the wild for over 130 years. Some experts consider that certain breeds of British pony might have some truly wild blood in them. The Exmoor just might be a true-blooded wild pony inhabiting a part of Britain that escaped the glaciation of the Ice Age, and there is speculation, too, about the Connemaras. Although the latter certainly has much Arab blood in it, horse skulls have been found in Irish peat bogs dating from a time just after the Ice Age and before domesticated horses are thought to have been used in Ireland.

LEFT: *The fortunes of the pony have greatly changed in Western countries. Once a beast of burden, now it is valued for its companionship and its important role in recreational riding.*

INTERBREEDING

Under natural conditions, wild equine species do not seem to interbreed. Even mountain zebras never cross with Butchell's zebras living in the same area. Grevy's zebras don't cross with wild asses in Somalia, nor onagers with Przewalski horses in Mongolia. Among domesticated animals, however, crosses do occur:

🔺 Male donkey x horse mare = mule
🔺 Female donkey x horse stallion = hinny
🔺 Zebra x horse = zebroid

All these hybrids, except for the occasional mule and zebra cross, are generally sterile although they are strong, amenable creatures. On the very rare occasions when they do breed successfully, a female mule crossed with a horse stallion produces either a mule or a horse, and the offspring of a female mule/male donkey cross will be either a true mule or a true ass. They never produce anything in between, because some of the eggs formed by the mule ovary are pure horse ones and others are pure donkey eggs. The eggs themselves are never hybrids.

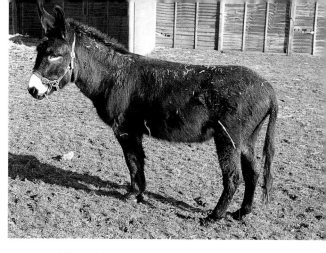

ABOVE: *Many young enthusiasts get their first taste of equine pleasures from the humble, delightful donkey.*

THE QUAGGA

Within living memory, one of the pony's wild relatives, a lovely, mysterious creature that looked half-zebra, half-pony, was made extinct by guess who? Man. This was the quagga of the South African plains. It had dark brown stripes on its head and neck, a brown body, and white legs and belly. Although claims to have seen specimens continued until as late as 1920, it is fairly certain that the last wild quagga was shot in 1861. They were said to emit a shrill bark.

Quaggas in captivity had thrived well—one was kept at Windsor Castle in the 1820s, and in 1860 a team of quaggas pulled a feed cart around London Zoo. The last quagga at Regent's Park died in 1872, and the last quagga in the world died in Amsterdam in 1883. Incredibly, but not uniquely (as witness the passing of the American passenger pigeon), no one attempted to breed quaggas in captivity; I suppose they assumed there would always be an abundance of wild quaggas in Africa. There are photographs of quaggas in existence, including the famous Stubbs painting of a quagga in the Royal College of Surgeons. About 20 quagga skins collect dust in the museums of the world. Let's hope that the wild horses and asses still clinging on to a precarious existence don't end up like that.

PIT PONIES

Up until recent years coal mines, especially those in South Wales, used ponies underground to pull loads of coal from the pit face to the shaft. These animals lived in perpetual gloom, covered in grime and dust, but generally were well treated by the miners who shared their subterranean labors with all the attendant dangers and deprivation.

Happily, there are now no more ponies living down in the mines; the last ones were brought to the surface to spend the rest of their lives in fresh air and sunlight. A number of rehabilitation centers for pit ponies, such as the one at Fforest Uchai Farm, in Wales, look after these brave little animals so deserving of a peaceful retirement.

ABOVE: *A most happy sight; a retired pit pony grazing in the sunlight, never to go underground ever again.*

HOW THE PONY EVOLVED

Ponies are built as we find them today, essentially because of a fundamental change in the Earth's climate that began about 24 million years ago. The weather became more distinctly and regularly seasonal, it was drier, and the tropical zone contracted toward the Equator. The forests began to retreat, and everywhere the plants that we call grasses became abundant. Open savannahs of grassland were established, and to take advantage of them, the horse descendants of *Hyracotherium* moved out of the bush. And, so that these creatures could cope with the benefits and dangers of the new wide-open spaces, evolution changed the structure of the equine body in various very sensible ways.

The three key requirements for life on the plains were as follows:

🔺 Efficient implements for cropping and grinding grass that, unlike the leaves on which the forest-living ancestors had lived, contains much harsh silica as well as more tough fiber—teeth.

🔺 Mechanisms for detecting trouble at a safe distance—senses.

🔺 Ways of avoiding trouble, now that the protective cover of the trees was forsaken—physique.

Horses, including modern ponies and donkeys, have all the right gear for doing these three things.

Teeth

The animals have two excellent types of teeth for dealing with grass: sharp incisors for cropping it, and special, high-crowned cheek teeth (molars and so on) for grinding it. Other grass eaters, such as cattle, sheep, and deer, digest fibrous food in their multichambered stomachs where they maintain colonies of useful digestive bacteria as slaves. Horses, ponies, and donkeys have relatively simple stomachs much more like humans', and possess very spacious large intestines in which bacteria also aid the digestive process.

Eyes and ears

Open spaces led to the evolution of large eyes that were set on the sides of the head, perfectly positioned to watch the horizon for any hint of danger while grazing. (Excellent hearing, with mobile, "direction-finding" ears, helps in the same way.)

The pony and donkey have excellent sight and can see a person at a distance of almost one mile. Because the eyes are set at the sides, the fields of vision of the two organs do not overlap and so they are unable to see stereoscopically, in 3-D, as we do. On the other hand, the horizontal, oblong pupil gives a far wider visual sweep of the distance than a round pupil would.

Although it cannot see as much of the spectrum as humans and other primates, the pony does have quite a wide range of color vision; in this respect, it is on a par with giraffes, sheep, and squirrels! Ponies can see much fine detail; their zebra cousins can recognize one another by the particular pattern of their stripes. Luckily, no two zebras have identical striping.

The mobile ears are used not just to catch sounds but also, particularly in wild horses, as a means of communication. They wag them to one another in a kind of simple semaphore.

The sense of smell is first class. The nostrils are large and supple and can be closed tightly against dust or sandstorms. In a good wind, a wild ass can scent a person at 500 yards (457 m).

Physique

Ponies have a larger body size than their ancient forest-dwelling ancestors; bulkier bodies both use food and conserve heat more efficiently. This increase in size was fine for animals that no longer had to slip under low-hanging branches.

To outdistance any attackers, the equines concentrated the immense power of their body muscles onto just four toes—one on each leg. The other toes were largely discarded so that the one that was left could be specially modified for superb running by elaborating the primitive "nail" into a hoof and devising a complex system of ligaments in the fetlock that increased flexibility on a fore-and-aft direction, decreased it from side to side, and so gave the leg much extra spring.

Domesticated ponies can be fairly fast movers but cannot rival their wild cousins. Wild asses can be remarkably swift and untiring, some experts considering them superior in some respects to riding-horses. Onagers, for example, have been timed running at an average of 28 mph (45 kph) for nearly half an hour with short bursts of over 30 mph (48 kph). Compare this with the record for a thoroughbred racehorse under ideal conditions over 3 miles (5 km) of 34.29 mph (55.18 kph). Even over a short distance, the racehorse is unlikely to surpass 40 mph (64 kph). The wild asses are no mean jumpers, either: onagers have cleared walls 7½ feet (3 m) high!

Finally, biologists put ponies fairly high on the animal scale of intelligence, and they are also believed to possess good memories. And one thing is certain: The humblest pony is as thoroughly equipped as a Derby winner with all the refinements that enabled horses to come galloping out of the jungle so many eons ago.

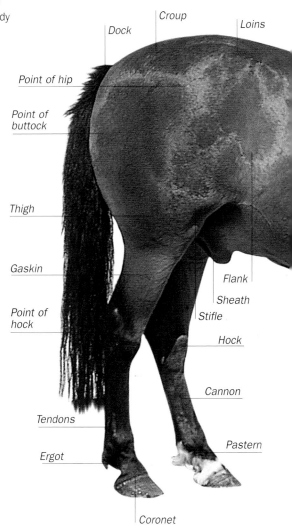

Croup

Dock

Loins

Point of hip

Point of buttock

Thigh

Gaskin

Flank

Sheath

Point of hock

Stifle

Hock

Cannon

Tendons

Pastern

Ergot

Coronet

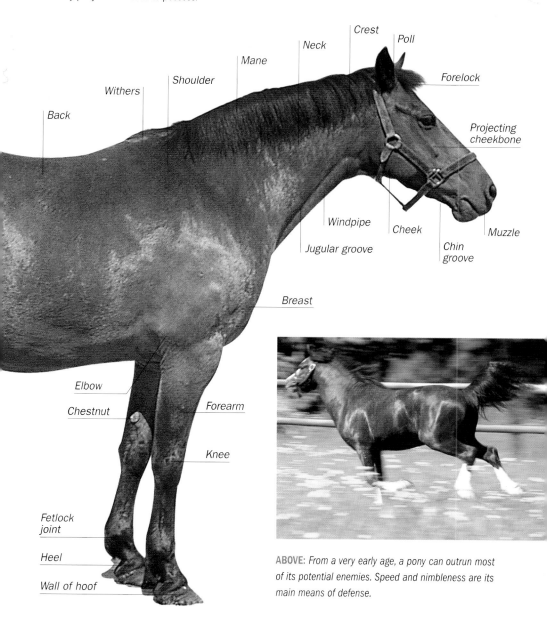

BELOW: *The points of a horse or pony; a vocabulary that every pony owner needs to possess.*

Crest

Poll

Neck

Mane

Forelock

Shoulder

Withers

Projecting cheekbone

Back

Windpipe

Cheek

Muzzle

Jugular groove

Chin groove

Breast

Elbow

Forearm

Chestnut

Knee

Fetlock joint

Heel

Wall of hoof

ABOVE: *From a very early age, a pony can outrun most of its potential enemies. Speed and nimbleness are its main means of defense.*

COMMON BRITISH BREEDS

At the beginning of the last century, Britain boasted 15 or more distinct pony breeds. Some of them, such as the Galloway, disappeared within living memory although their blood lives on in many Highland and Fell ponies. Today the native pony breeds of Great Britain, usually called mountain and moorland ponies, although they are by no means located solely in or adapted to the uplands, are nine in number. Stud books and regulation of standards are maintained for each breed. The nine breeds are as follows:

NEW FOREST PONIES

This breed comes in all sorts of colors, although piebald and skewbald ponies are considered to be "impure." They inhabit the Crown forest that gives them their name and that lies in Hampshire between the River Avon and Southampton Water. Their breeding is controlled by the selection of stallions that are caught and shown every April, inferior specimens being weeded out. The mares run free all year-round, tending to stay in particular parts of the forest that can be regarded as their home, in groups of between one and six with their offspring. The ponies are good for the forest itself; their movements and grazing stop the woodland from becoming choked with undergrowth.

BELOW: *This chestnut New Forest pony stallion is a superb specimen.*

DARTMOOR PONIES

These resemble New Forest ponies but, because the stallions are not selected systematically as they are for the New Forest breed, they come in an even greater range of varieties. They have small heads with very small ears and stand between 11 and 12.2 hands. The colors are normally bay, black, brown, or gray; again, piebalds and skewbalds are taboo. Dartmoor ponies are kind and easily tamed.

EXMOOR PONIES

True Exmoors, unlike other British ponies, are uniform in appearance: they are dark brown in color with little or no white. They have a light-colored muzzle; a broad forehead; short, thick ears; nice big eyes;

ABOVE: A Dartmoor pony stallion. Its head is somewhat smaller than those of most other pony breeds.

BELOW: This Exmoor pony is showing its overall uniform dark brown coat.

a deep barrel-like chest; fine legs; and a rather harsh, springy coat. They stand about 12.2 hands high. A hand is 4 inches (10 cm), so 12.2 hands is 50 inches (125 cm). They are very rugged and have been known to survive unusually severe winters that killed off sheep and even deer. It is possible that the Exmoor is Britain's only truly pure wild horse. Some experts even consider it to be the only pure-blooded wild horse still existing in the world—this

BELOW: *This Connemara pony is plainly carrying some Arab characteristics.*

school of thought believes the Przewalski horse to be a crossbreed. Certainly the Exmoor area escaped glaciation during the Ice Age, and in the Mendip Caves have been discovered fossilized remains, dated as being around 100,000 years old and identical to modern Exmoor ponies.

CONNEMARA PONIES

This docile breed comes from the hills of Galway in Ireland. It also occurs in many colors, has a deep, chunky body and short legs, and stands 13–14.2 hands. Lots of Arab blood flows through its veins and it is a fearless little jumper.

WELSH PONIES

These ponies come in all colors and have a heavy head with a short mane and tail. There may be true British wild pony blood in them, but mostly they are descended from Oriental breeds that were imported by the Romans.

SHETLAND PONIES

They may be small (around 10.2 hands) but Shetlands are tough and strong. They have broad chests and hindquarters, lovely flowing manes and tails, small ears, and large, well-spaced eyes. Colors are variable, but black is particularly popular. Shetlands still live outside all year. Selective breeding and control of the type did not begin until the late nineteenth century under the auspices of Lord Londonderry in Great Britain.

ABOVE: *The fearless and reliable Shetland pony.*
BELOW: *A Welsh pony of the Welsh Cob or Welsh Section D type; an excellent all-rounder.*

HIGHLAND PONIES

There is plenty of variety in this tough little breed. They are stocky animals with little ears, flowing manes and tails, and long hair around the feet. Their eyes are set well apart and they come in a wide range of colors, including chestnut with a silver mane and tail. They may show "zebra stripes" on the knees and hocks. Standing between 12.2–14.2 hands, the heavier representatives tend to be found on the Scottish mainland (they are called garrons) and the lighter ones on the Western Isles. They possess plenty of Arab and French pony blood.

DALES PONIES

Dales ponies originate from the northern counties of England and the neighboring lowland areas of Scotland. They were important pack animals essential to commerce for hundreds of years right up until the nineteenth century. They stand up to 15 hands and are more massively built than Fell ponies. Their color is mainly black, although not quite as much as in Fell ponies, and white markings are permissible.

FELL PONIES

Originating from the same general areas as Dales ponies, the Fells were essentially riding animals used on the uplands, whereas the heavier Dales had their place in the valleys where industry and trade were centered. Fell ponies are mainly black with a small number of browns, bays, and grays. They stand up to 14.2 hands and trot fast and tirelessly. The presence of foreign blood in their makeup (Friesian, Dolehest, and Fjord pony) recalls the settlement of England's northern counties at various times in history by invaders from the Low Countries and Norway.

OPPOSITE TOP: *Dales ponies were originally used as pack animals for carrying loads of lead.*
OPPOSITE BOTTOM: *A Fell pony. These ponies came originally from the west of the Pennines, whereas the Dale ponies came from the east of those hills.*
BELOW: *A fine gray Highland pony. The smaller Highlands are found on the Western Isles.* .

COMMON AMERICAN BREEDS

After the mysterious disappearance of horses from the Americas in around 6000 B.C.E., over 7,000 years passed before these animals were reintroduced by the Spanish colonists. Much credit for the conquistadors' success must be given to their four-legged companions, not least because of the way in which the appearance of these unknown "monster" creatures instilled fear into the indigenous peoples confronted by the invaders. Thereafter, over the centuries, with the arrival of immigrants and their equines from every part of the world, different types of specifically American horses and ponies were developed

by artificial selection. Some breeds are of relatively recent origin.

PONY OF THE AMERICAS

It was in 1954 that Les Boomhower, a breeder of Shetland ponies in Iowa, obtained an Arab/Appaloosa mare that had accidentally been mated with a Shetland stallion. When the foal was born it turned out to be a delightful little character with black smudges all over his body. Named Black Hand by Boomhower, this was the first Pony of the Americas (POA). The new breed was quickly established, standards were set by the POA

BELOW: *Around for less than 50 years, the Pony of the Americas is an attractive animal, perfect for beginners.*

Club, and the new ponies became a roaring success. They have a variety of coat patterns, the most common being the so-called blanket pattern—white loins and limbs with dark round markings that can range in size from mere specks to patches of 4 inches (10 cm) or more in diameter. Some have spots all over the body—the leopard pattern.

Other characteristics are mottled skin (also found in the Appaloosa), a very visible white sclera (the white opaque part of the eyeball), and closely defined light or dark vertical stripes on the hooves (occasionally to be seen also in other breeds).

The POA is a gentle and easily trainable breed—intelligent, durable, and of a steady temperament, it is the ideal pony for beginners.

OCRACOKE PONY (BANTER PONY)

Ocracoke Island off the North Carolina coast is home to a pony breed whose origins lie in a variety of romantic legends. Some say these ponies are the descendants of horses brought from Spain by Cortez as he searched for gold while exploring eastward to Mexico. Others prefer a story of a ship carrying a circus and all its animals that sank in a storm, all perishing with the exception of two horses. Experts believe that the most probable ancestors of the breed were ponies brought with the Raleigh expeditions that were left on Roanoke Island at the time of the mysterious lost colony. These ponies, which are protected by the National Park Service, roam 160 acres (65 ha) of Ocracoke Island.

CHINCOTEAGUE PONY

Assateague Island, 37 miles (60 km) long, lies off the coast of Maryland and Virginia. The ponies living there are feral animals, descendants of domesticated animals that have reverted to the wild. Where did they come from? Some say a shipwrecked Spanish galleon, but more probably they are descended from horses brought to the island in the seventeenth century by owners living on the mainland who were anxious to avoid livestock taxes.

The Chincoteague "pony" may well be a "horse" that averages only 12–13 hands in height due to the low-quality food supply and inclement environment. These ponies survive on coarse salt marsh grasses, twigs, and seaweeds and drink very salty, brackish water.

Two main herds live on the island—one at the Maryland end, the other at the Virginia end. Each state manages its own herd and, by selling excess stock and administering contraceptive drugs by flying darts, keeps their numbers down to a maximum of 150 per herd.

AMERICAN WALKING PONY

This breed was developed in the 1960s from a foundation of Tennessee Walking Horse and Welsh Pony. From the former it inherited an elegant, smooth saddle gait; from the latter an exquisite head and long, arched neck. The various Walking Pony gaits are passed down from generation to generation and they include the delightfully named Pleasure Walk and the Merry Walk. Riding these ponies with their ability to move smoothly and change lightly from one gait to another is truly memorable.

QUARTER PONY

This popular, even-tempered pony is a mini Quarter Horse, developed from some of the latter that did not attain the American Quarter Horse Association's original minimum height requirement of 14.2 hands. Unlike its larger relative, it comes in a variety of colors.

On average, most Quarter Ponies are about 13.2 hands and are excellent for small riders, although bigger, heavily muscled ponies are now being raised. These powerful animals make fine mounts for large riders and can commonly be seen at country events, taking part in steer wrestling competitions ("bulldogging").

CAYUSE INDIAN PONY

Less well known than the POA, and nowadays found mostly in California, this small and steady pony with high withers and unusually long cannon bones is probably a descendant of French horses brought to Canada in the seventeenth century. Later, Pawnee Indians crossed these European ponies with lighter-built Spanish Arabs, producing a tough, fast-running pony with unbounded stamina. By the early 1800s, as a result of careful selective breeding by the Cayuse Indians, the Cayuse Indian Pony was a separate breed, notable for its colorful coat with a tendency toward abundant white markings or spots.

BELOW: *The Cayuse Indian pony was developed by Native Americans from European pony stock.*

OTHER PONY BREEDS

Across the world there are several hundred distinct breeds of pony—some in abundance, some extremely rare. As well as providing pure riding pleasure for people of all ages, they may also be found carrying farmers and shepherds as they go about their work, as beasts of burden and pullers of wheeled vehicles, in specialist roles in the game of polo or the wild races of the Mongolian steppes, and even, in some places, as providers of milk! Watch for these breeds on your travels and ask the locals about them. Here are just a few.

BELOW: *The tiny Falabella pony whose origins are most mysterious.*

Avelignese: A pack pony from the Alps and Appenines of Italy.

Balearic: A rare working pony that you may be lucky enough to see in the orange groves of Majorca in the Balearic Islands.

Bashirsky: A pony breed from Russia whose mares produce milk that is drunk for its medicinal properties. One mare can produce over 400 gallons (1818 L) of milk during a "milking season" of seven months.

Bosnian: A super-tough, intelligent, multi-purpose pony from Yugoslavia.

Camarguais: The famous gray-white pony of the marshes of France. It has one more lumbar vertebra (seven) than most other horses.

Dulmen: A disappearing breed from the Westphalian area of Germany.

Falabella: The smallest horse in the world, which stands under 28 inches (70 cm) high. It has to look up at a Great Dane! There are various fables as to how the breed originated from a strange dwarf horse that wandered out of the South American jungle years ago, but the facts seem to be that it is the result of selective

inbreeding by the Falabella family of Recreo de Roca Ranch, near Buenos Aires, from the offspring of an original Shetland pony/thoroughbred cross. You can see these diminutive but hardy creatures at some stables and wildlife parks around the world.

Galiceno: A breed brought to Mexico from Spain by the explorer Cortez and now popular throughout the United States. It is gentle by nature and an excellent child's pony.

Garrano: The Portuguese pony, unchanged since the times of cavemen's drawings.

Haflinger: A mountain expert for the Austrian Tyrol, this pony is a strong worker up to an age of 35 years or more!

Manipur: The traditional breed in Assam. Polo was played on them as early as 625 c.e.

Marwari: The cavalry pony of the Mogul emperors of India.

Sable Island: A breed of only 200–300 ponies, descended from the eighteenth-century New England breeds. These ponies live with little shelter on the bleak, barren

Sable Island, off the coast of Nova Scotia.

Sandalwood: A fast racer that hails from the Indonesian lands of Sumbra al Sumbrawa.

Senner: A native German breed. Some are said to be living still truly wild in the forests around Bielefeld.

Spiti: A tough, high-altitude mountain climber from the Himalayas.

Taishuh: A strong, rugged pony from Japan, it dates back to the eighth century. Only about 70 of them now exist.

Vyatka: A tough Russian pony in need of protection as its numbers are now no more than 2,000. In the nineteenth century, this handsome pony was considered to be the best troika horse in Russia.

Yonaguni: Another rare pony that is native to the southwest islands of Japan. Usually chestnut in color, gentle by nature, and very strong, its ancestors arrived on the islands at about the time of Christ.

BELOW: *The Haflinger pony was bred for hard work in the mountains of the Austrian Tyrol.*

CHAPTER TWO

ACQUIRING YOUR PONY

Acquiring a good pony that is sound and of pleasing conformation is a potential minefield for the unwary. While the majority of pony vendors are honest and often knowledgeable, some unscrupulous horse dealers also lurk in the undergrowth. Of course, you may be giving a good home to a poor old thing rescued by an animal rights group or horse protection organization. If you are taking on such an animal, three cheers for you and you'll undoubtedly be well rewarded. However, if you are purchasing the animal, beware. The world is full of pitfalls for the pony buyer and you need to follow the guidelines on the next few pages.

CHOOSING A PONY

Acquiring a pony should never be undertaken lightly. Before deciding to proceed and making your choice of animal, there are some important considerations to be taken into account by you and your family.

YOUR CIRCUMSTANCES

Do you have access to stabling and good or poor grazing? Do you have someone who can care for the pony while you're away on vacation?

A tough, native breed pony on good grazing with shelter will need less food than a more delicate "blue-blood" pony on sparser grazing—up to 75 percent less! It is more expensive to have a pony boarded out at a livery stable.

WHAT KIND OF PONY?

What sort of pony do you want and for what purposes? Native breeds are cheaper to keep, hardier, and generally easier to handle than thoroughbred ones. Riding school ponies are understandably more stoical and amenable, by and large, than privately owned (sometimes spoiled!) ones. Gelding ponies are somewhat more placid than mares.

WHAT SIZE PONY?

Young people grow faster than ponies. In general, a sturdy 14.2 pony will carry children and adults of most sizes but do try it out by sitting on it. The only rule is: Does it feel right?

WHAT AGE PONY?

Not too young and inexperienced, not too old and fixed in its (possibly undesirable) ways. I believe a good age is seven to nine years. A pony that old is usually about to enter its best years and will steadily improve until it is approaching 20. Even after that, although perhaps with less vigor than before, the animal can give you at least 10 years or more. The better you keep the pony, the longer its active life. Very old ponies can be just the thing for small or more nervous children.

LEFT: It is vital to try out a pony for size and "fit" by riding it before buying. Does it feel right for YOU?

COST OF MAINTENANCE

Can you afford the costs of routine maintenance of a pony? As well as food (and perhaps grazing) costs and stabling (or livery) fees, you must also budget for insurance, veterinary fees (hopefully your pony will remain healthy, but even so there will be annual protective vaccination against tetanus and flu, and worming several times a year), the cost of tack and equipment, and hoof trimming and shoeing by the blacksmith between two and eight times a year.

WHERE TO OBTAIN YOUR PONY

You may be lucky enough to be offered a pony that you know well by a friend or your local riding school. Pony protection societies frequently look for good homes where they can place (lend rather than sell) their rescued animals. Then there are advertisements in the horse magazines as well as pony dealers and pony auctions. When assessing a potential purchase, it is essential for you to get the guidance and good advice of someone with experience—a member of the pony club, your riding school, a blacksmith, or another established pony owner. But besides that, whatever you do, before you part with any cash, have the pony "vetted" by your veterinarian, a process for which you will have to pay a fee but that will be money well spent.

WHAT SHOULD YOU EXPECT?

First, you should look at the pony.
🔺 Is it alert, bright, interested in you?
🔺 Is it calm and amenable when approached and touched?
🔺 Are its movements fluid and easy?
🔺 How does it react to saddling up, to being ridden?
🔺 Ride the pony yourself. Does it go

ABOVE: *Have the pony walked around so that you can assess its movement and temperament.*

smoothly and willingly or is it sluggish and awkward?
🔺 Have it trotted away from and then toward you. Does it nod its head when one but not the other forefoot takes the weight? This action may indicate lameness. Is each hind foot placed equally firmly, and for the same length of time, on the ground—if not, again, there could be some lameness.
🔺 Have the pony walked in a tight circle, while on a lead rein or halter, first clockwise and then counterclockwise. Does it turn smoothly without stumbling? When backed up, does it do so without protest and free of any exaggerated action of the hind legs?
🔺 If possible, see the pony out on the road. What is it like when close to traffic—skittish or as cool as a cucumber?

INSPECT THE PONY

The first rule is to make sure that you have the animal inspected thoroughly before you hand over any cash. Get someone who really knows horses, preferably your own veterinarian, to go over the animal. Everything has to be sound and in good working order, even if the conformation—the shape and makeup of the animal—may be imperfect, unpretty, or unbalanced aesthetically in some respects. In a pet for the enthusiastic young rider, conformation and looks should not normally be of great concern, provided that any points of bad conformation do not represent areas of potentially weak anatomy. Horse terms concerned with conformation include "goose rump" (quarters that drop

RIGHT: *Check the pony's hooves for trapped stones, frog trouble, and splits in the walls.*

EXAMINING THE PONY

Although the veterinarian will carry out a detailed examination, you should try to check certain things yourself. Find out the answers to some questions. What is the pony's age? Is the conformation of the animal satisfactory? What is its height?

Run your hands over the body and legs. Are there any odd lumps or bumps or scars in the saddle area or on the limbs? Does the pony resent being touched anywhere? Pick up a foreleg and then a hind leg, handle the tail, moving it gently from side to side—is the pony happy to oblige? Do the hooves look in good condition? Check for signs of overgrowth of the hoof, uneven wear, or horizontal ridges and grooves on the hoof wall that may indicate past bouts of laminitis. Is the frog of each foot well formed and the sole gently arched? Stand back and look at the pony's legs. Does each foreleg and each hind leg match the one on the other side?

In all of this, take your time. Don't rush to make a decision. Pay attention to your gut feelings—do you like the pony; does it like you; do you both "click"?

steeply to the tail), "toad eye" (prominent eyes), and "cow hocks" (hocks that lean in toward one another). However, a little bit of any of these doesn't automatically mean that the pony is unsound or likely to be anything but a great deal of fit fun.

Some points of conformation are obviously undesirable because they probably signify trouble. For example, "boxy feet"—steep, narrow, punched-in hooves—can be just asking for lameness, and a "ewe neck," which, like that of a shorn sheep, is concave on its upper edge, may suggest neck muscles that are not as flexible as they should be and could cause schooling and balance problems.

RIGHT: The correct position for checking the foreleg.

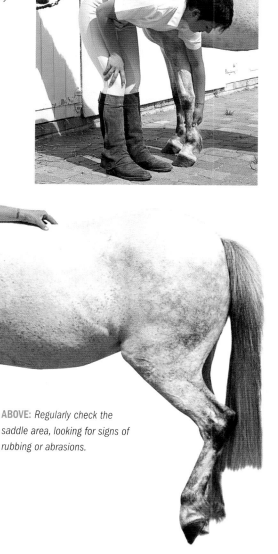

ABOVE: Regularly check the saddle area, looking for signs of rubbing or abrasions.

DETAILED EXAMINATION

The animal generally should be compact and neat, with a head in proportion to its body. When you are examining the pony, check the points that are listed here so that you are satisfied that its health and conformation are sound. Better still, as advised, get your veterinarian or an expert to check the pony over for you.

Withers and back

Check for strange swellings on the withers and for saddle-produced sores or scars. The back must be neither arched ("roached") nor sunken, but straight and neither too long nor too short. The withers should be inconspicuous and the quarters should continue evenly the line of the back and then slope gracefully without sudden angling to the tailhead.

Coat

Check the health of the skin and hair, and its freedom from skin disease and parasites. Check all over the body for warts, wounds, bumps, lumps, and other oddities.

Tail

Check the hair for any indications of disease or old injuries.

Hooves

All hooves should be well formed and intact, with good soles and frogs (V-shaped pads on the soles): check the wall, sole, and frog of each hoof for cleanliness and absence of disease.

Chest

The chest ought to be deep in relation to the distance between it and the ground, and the ribs well sprung. Check that the chest movements are smooth and unlabored.

Eyes

These should be large and amiable. Check for normal anatomy and function. Any discharge? The veterinarian may look into each eye with an ophthalmoscope.

Ears

Check for activity, good voluntary mobility, and absence of discharge.

Neck

This should not be lean or scrawny.

Nostrils

These should be wide. Check for size and absence of discharge.

Mouth

Check the teeth for age (see page 40), alignment, and condition of both the incisors and molars. Can they chomp up hay efficiently? The incisors should meet exactly. Check for gum disease and gum color.

Legs

There should be four legs! Each foreleg must be so straight that a vertical line would run from the point of the shoulder down through the center of the limb and its foot. A vertical line from the point of the buttocks should likewise bisect the hind leg and foot. Pasterns and hocks must not slope too much. There should be no scars, abnormal swellings, tender areas, bumps, or lumps on any limb, and the feet should be turned neither inward like a pigeon's nor out like a duck's. In a nutshell, the legs must be clean, neat, bold, and strong.

The pony's chest

The veterinarian will listen to the heart and lung sounds with a stethoscope. No coughing should be present; beware the tale, "Oh, he's only coughing because I stirred up some dust in the stable when I opened a bale of hay five minutes ago."

You can feel the heartbeat with your hand and hear it by pressing your head against the pony's chest on the left side at the point of the elbow; the pulse is usually taken under one branch of the lower jaw. The heart rate of ponies at rest is about 45 beats per minute (newborn foals about 90 per minute). The rate gradually decreases throughout the first year of life. An occasional missed beat is not uncommon in healthy animals, but the veterinarian will look for the cause. Breathing should be silent and regular when resting, with about 10–12 breaths per minute. This may increase to 80 or even 100 breaths per minute after intensive exertion.

After examining the chest at rest, the veterinarian will want the pony exercised quickly for a short time to see what happens to the pulse and to hear the breathing rate. A fit animal rapidly returns to normal after some exertion. Failure to do so may indicate lung or heart trouble.

Droppings

Check for consistency, color, smell, and general appearance. Is there any evidence of undigested food? There may be no obvious worms, but this can and must be confirmed, preferably before or at least as soon as possible after purchase, by asking the veterinarian to do a microscopic examination of the droppings. This is very important in donkeys, which often carry lungworms. If they are to be companions to ponies, check their droppings first for signs of lungworms so they can receive regular worming if necessary and thus avoid cross-infection. Ponies do pass wind from time to time. Excessive or very frequent flatulence may indicate indigestion. Ignore rumbling tummy noises to be heard in the abdominal area.

Urine

Check the color. There is a variety of colors and consistencies of normal equine urine. Often, perfectly healthy urine contains a white or creamy sludge. Black or obviously bloody urine needs immediate veterinary attention.

Demeanor

Is the animal alert, perky, and interested in everything going on around him? He should not be listless and dull.

Movement

Does the pony move freely and easily without a stilted or abnormal gait? The veterinarian will want to watch someone walk, trot, and perhaps canter and gallop the pony. He or she will want to see it backed up and turned in tight clockwise and counterclockwise circles. All or any of these movements may reveal lameness or faults in gait, balance, or coordination. When walking or trotting the pony, don't hold the halter rope too close to the head to give it plenty of rope. Look ahead of you as you lead it toward, across the front of, or away from the veterinarian. If it's for riding, see it saddled and harnessed. Check the fit of all the equipment—are there any points of pinching, rubbing, or irritation?

Behavior

Watch the animal's behavior in its familiar environment. How does it feed? Are there any signs of vices—bad habits that can be difficult to eradicate and debilitating to the pony? The veterinarian should pick up signs of these vices during the physical examination, but others are trickier to detect and may need time and observation of the animal's behavior in its stable. Vices include "crib biting" (chewing anything within reach, particularly woodwork), "wind sucking" (swallowing air), and "weaving" (a repetitive rocking from side to side). They tend to manifest themselves only in the stable, not when the animal is out at pasture.

FINALLY...

If you are finally satisfied and decide to buy your pony, try to get it on approval for as long as possible. Try also to get a warranty certifying full soundness, signed by a qualified veterinarian. Make sure that you have any vaccination certificates relating to your pet. When you take it back to its new home, let it familiarize itself with its surroundings for a day or so before riding it. If you have other equines, don't mix them immediately—let them get to know each other for a day or two, separated by a stable half-door or a fence.

INSURANCE

Ponies are best insured against accidental death, veterinary fees, loss of use, and third-party risks. Several insurance companies offer policies but premium rates and conditions vary, so check and compare first.

Sadly, ponies are sometimes stolen. A powerful deterrent to such thefts is freeze branding. This entails putting a permanent number on the animal's skin by way of an iron cooled in liquid nitrogen. This method of branding is completely humane and is available from a number of companies advertising in horse magazines.

BELOW: *These two friends are enjoying themselves in the summer sunshine. Pony ownership confers certain responsibilities but it's well worth it.*

AGING

Telling the age of a pony can be easier in some cases than others. It is not an exact science and is more prone to error at certain ages. Like some secondhand car dealers, unscrupulous sellers of horseflesh can attempt to "doctor" the age of their wares, even by actually tampering with the physical appearance of the animal's teeth. However, what is tolerated in the case of movie stars, actresses, and the like—the majority of whom suspend the laws of time around the age of 21—is definitely not permissible when you, the innocent purchaser, are looking for a long-eared and four-footed friend.

There is nothing wrong as such with a pony that has passed middle age or even trotted into old age, but you certainly should know how old your pony is. One method is to look at its teeth.

So what are horse folks doing when they grab a mean hold on their mount's tongue (not at all a painful procedure, although it looks most undignified) and stare, nodding wisely, into the horse's mouth? They are looking at certain features of the teeth—numbers, types, shapes, marks—all of which give clues (accurate up to eight years and somewhat less so up to about 30 years of age) as to how many birthdays their equine has seen. The technique is the same in horses, ponies, and donkeys.

TEETH

Ponies generally have 42 teeth, composed of:
- Twelve incisors (front teeth)
- Four tushes (canine or fang teeth)
- Twenty-four cheek teeth (molars)
- Two rudimentary molars called "wolf teeth"

Both "milk" and permanent sets of incisors and cheek teeth are to be found in the pony and donkey, but only tushes and wolf teeth (when present) are permanent. Milk teeth are somewhat triangular, shell-like and lighter colored than the more oblong, yellower, heavier-built permanent teeth. Mares rarely grow their tushes, and often ponies don't produce wolf teeth either.

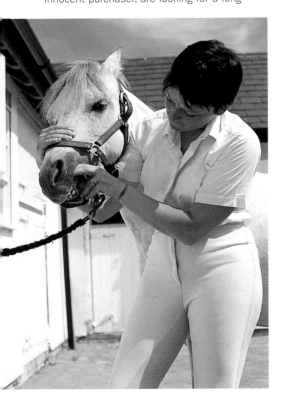

LEFT: *The correct way of inspecting a pony's teeth in order to try and assess its age.*

In the United States, it is traditional to take January 1 as the official birthday of all thoroughbreds. (In Britain, May 1 is considered the official birthday of all equines.) That is the base point from which tooth checks are judged. For aging, we can ignore the developments in the cheek teeth and concentrate solely on the incisors, whose positions in each jaw are termed central, lateral, and corner.

How the teeth change

At birth, the foal has two central milk incisors in upper and lower jaw.

At one month, the lateral incisors appear but don't meet their opposite numbers until five months. At this time, the corner incisors can be felt preparing to poke through the gums.

At one year, the corner incisors are well through but don't touch their fellows in the opposite jaw until one-and-a-half years.

At two years, all six upper incisors are perfectly aligned and touching the lower six. The central milk incisors are beginning to loosen at the gum.

At two-and-a-half years, the permanent central incisors push out their milk predecessors but don't meet.

At three years, they do.

At three-and-a-half years, the permanent laterals are through but not meeting. Tushes may appear in the males about now.

At four years, the permanent laterals meet.

At four-and-a-half years, the permanent corner teeth arrive on the scene.

At five years, all permanent incisors are through and meeting with the corners just so. Also at five years, the incisors possess in their wearing surfaces distinct dark hollows called "marks."

At six years, each incisor shows a smooth ring of worn tooth around its mark. The marks on the central incisors begin to fade in their intensity.

At seven years, the central and lateral marks are smaller, shallower, and paler than on the corner teeth. A "hook" develops on the upper corner teeth.

At eight years, the marks on all the teeth are faint and shallow. The hook has almost or completely gone.

At nine years, a groove, Galvayne's groove, first appears on the upper corner incisor teeth. It steadily moves down the teeth and is halfway down at 15, fully down at 20, halfway out (only present in the lower half of the tooth) at 25, and is gone by 30 years. The length and position of Galvayne's groove is your best guide in the years between nine and 30, although experts also note changes in the tooth tables (wearing surfaces) and the angle of the teeth. Basically, as the years progress, the shape of the tooth tables change. Also, whereas, say, lower incisors are fairly upright at 10 years of age, projecting at an angle of around 45 degrees above the horizontal, by the age of 30 they are leaning outward at only 25 degrees.

ON SAFARI

Wild asses and zebras can be aged in the same way as ponies, but zebras go through the various stages roughly six months ahead of their domesticated cousins. I do not recommend that you try grabbing a zebra's tongue in order to practice your aging skills when you next visit the local zoo or go on safari in Kenya.

CHAPTER THREE

FEEDING AND DIET

The correct feeding of your pony is much more than the provision of calories to fuel the riding and other activities of the animal. Tip-top health, good condition, and smart appearance, as well as the steady growth and development of younger ponies, vitally depend upon it. No less than other fuel costs in the modern world, that of the pony continues to rise. The fueling of our long-eared friends cannot be done cheaply and demands constant, careful attention. As well as the right quantities of various foodstuffs, the pony's well-being depends on being fed nutrients of only the highest quality.

THE PONY'S NATURAL DIET

The ancestors of the pony were incredibly hardy beasts, and today its closest living wild relatives survive in some of the most inhospitable regions of the world where food is generally low in both quantity and quality. The Przewalski horse, which at usually less than 14 hands in height should really be classified as a pony, hails from the high steppes of Mongolia and Dzungaria, rocky, arid country bordering the Gobi Desert, which is dry and hot in summer and bitterly cold in winter. The Przewalskis wander in search of tussock grass, tamarisk, wormwood, and saxaul shrubs, which, though dry looking, possess a juicy bark that the animals strip. They might go three or four days without water and in summer dig holes in the soil with their hooves, searching for a little salty water.

Kiangs come across good feed during only two months of the year, August and September, and have learned to cope with the harsh swamp grass that is packed with silica and would cut the more sensitive mouths of their domesticated cousins to pieces. In January and February, they get their water requirements by eating snow, apparently without harm. Onagers root around in the deserts for any grasses or plants that can grow in the scorched and barren wilderness. They survive by cropping over 100 varieties of edible plants, which absorb moisture from the atmosphere during the cool nights, and by eating a fair quantity of the salty soil of their environment. African wild asses, denizens of regions where the temperature may reach 122°F (50°C), need to do plenty of grazing in order to fill their stomachs from the lean pickings of the parched, rocky landscape. They are up early, foraging at daybreak, then resting in the heat of the day, and feeding again from around 5:00 P.M. until sunset. Happily, our domesticated ponies don't have to put up with that sort of life. Today's pony feeds well and healthily and should know nothing of hunger, thirst, and hard times. However, the cost of animal foodstuffs everywhere rises steadily in the face of ever-growing demand from meat- and grain-eating human populations.

OPPOSITE: *Ponies doing what comes naturally. This pair will be fully nourished by a pasture plainly in excellent condition.*

THE IDEAL DIET

The quantity and makeup of your pony's ration will depend on the following:

🔺 Whether or not it is grazing
🔺 Its size and body weight
🔺 The amount of work it does

Adjustment of each particular ration is necessary after experience has shown whether or not an animal does well on what it is given. Some individuals need a little more concentrated food than others in order to stay perky and in good condition; other ponies need a little less to prevent them from becoming too belligerent and fiery.

Under ideal natural conditions, a pony would obtain all the nutrients it needs from the variety of plant life in the pastures on which it grazes. "Grass" in such a case is far more than the green stubbly stuff that Dad mows on a Sunday afternoon; indeed, it is a remarkable variety of vegetation containing weeds, seeds, flowers, shoots, stems, leaves, and bits of soil that contribute the necessary carbohydrates, protein, fats, minerals, and vitamins. However, most ponies are not kept on ideal pasture, or they graze for only part of the year. Many are kept in paddocks where there is little either in quality or quantity of plant growth. Others are stabled permanently.

Important: For information on poisonous types of vegetation, see page 59.

BELOW: *This pony is in tip-top condition. Health and condition vitally depend on correct feeding.*

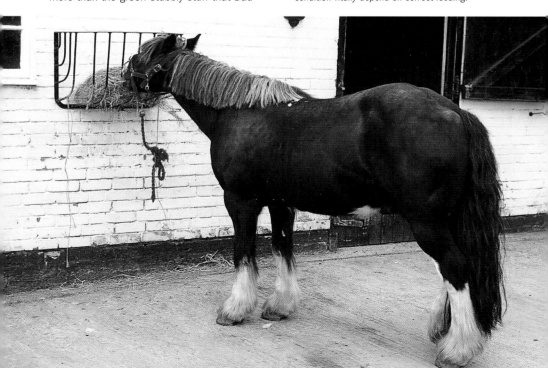

BULK FOODS

🔺 **Hay:** There are many varieties of hay and it is important to obtain and feed good-quality stuff that is more nutritious and won't make your pet ill. Hay that hasn't "cured" correctly after cutting can cause lung and kidney irritation as well as intestinal upsets. Good hay smells like a newly mowed meadow, contains leaves of a pale pastel green, and has flowerheads still attached to the stalks. Hay that is crumbly and smells musty, or is damp and sour in parts of the bale, or is very dusty, or is obviously affected here and there with whitish mold, or is dark brown and smells like tobacco, should be rejected.

🔺 **Commercial concentrates:** Feed companies make a premixed feed for every need, from foals to older horses. Some contain both roughages and concentrates.

🔺 **Bran:** This is a traditional horse dish, although it isn't very much liked by our equine friends, and nowadays, because modern milling methods have removed the flour it once contained, it has little food value. Its mineral content is not well balanced; there is too much phosphorus and not enough calcium in most samples of bran. Feeding an excessive amount of bran can lead to bone diseases, such as Big Head or Miller's Disease. Nevertheless, it does provide fibrous bulk and therefore can be used for its mild laxative effect, made up as a mash (see box).

🔺 **Root vegetables:** Carrots, turnips, and beets provide bulk, sugars, and vitamins. They must, however, be clean and free of rotten parts. Chop them up before serving. Beet pulp must never be fed dry; it will swell up in the pony's intestines and can cause colic, choking, and even death. The pulp must always be soaked in water for at least six hours before feeding.

BRAN MASH

2 pounds (1 kg) bran

1/2 ounce (15 g) salt

1 1/2 pints (900 ml) boiling water

Mix well together and cover with a plate or thick cloth pressed well down onto the mash. Leave for 30 minutes and then feed when cool enough. To increase its appeal to ponies that usually regard it in rather the way that a diner at an expensive restaurant would cast an eye over an unsolicited bowl of cold porridge, add a couple of tablespoons of syrup, molasses, or oats. Bran mash quickly goes sour, so always use it freshly made.

ENERGY-PRODUCING FEEDS

These feeds provide the rich food that is necessary for a pony that does work, in the winter and at other times when grazing is greatly reduced or absent.

🔺 **Oats:** The best-known energy food for equines is, of course, oats. The richness in calories of this sort of grain is accepted in common parlance; its ability to produce friskiness has led to phrases such as "he cannot carry his corn" for someone who becomes less restrained after reaching prosperity, and "he's feeling his oats" for a lively individual. Whole oats should be pleasant smelling, dry, light in color, and free from dust. Moldy oats smell "off," produce dust, or are faintly damp and can produce illnesses, ranging from chest trouble to kidney disease. Crushed and rolled oats are produced from whole oats by machinery that breaks the outer husk of the oats. The idea is to allow digestive juices more ready access to the nourishing, carbohydrate-rich interior. However, a normal pony can grind whole oats perfectly satisfactorily, and there can be difficulty in spotting substandard samples of oats after they have been broken by the machinery. All the same, I tend to prefer crushed oats and would advise, if possible, that you check the quality of some whole oats before buying and then have that batch processed. Crushed and rolled oats are particularly suitable for older animals, invalids, and beasts with imperfect teeth.

FIBER

All energy foods need to be fed along with fiber-containing or bulk foods in order to be sure that they are properly digested. The intestines of the pony are specially designed to do the job of breaking down the tough cellulose walls that surround the inner, nutritious parts of plant material. Whereas cattle, sheep, giraffes, and other cud-chewing animals do this by means of an internal population of friendly digesting bacteria stored in four stomachs, our equine friends store the bacteria in greatly enlarged intestines. To function properly, these cavernous organs need plenty of fiber for the worker bacteria to perch on while working and to stimulate gentle contractions of the intestine wall.

Pony cubes and horse nuts: These compounded foods are actually mixtures in pellet form made from dried grass, hay, and grains with the addition of minerals and vitamins. They are carefully made to strict specifications and can form a complete diet. Their advantages are simplicity, scientific balance, freedom from dustiness, and ease of storage. Their disadvantages are cost and low roughage content. Animals fed nothing but nuts or cubes tend to root for roughage, and this may range from eating their bedding to slowly demolishing their surroundings by chomping at any available woodwork. Coarse mixes ("sweetfeeds") are compressed feeds that are flaked rather than ground and cubed. Other energy foods are peas, beans, and flaked corn. Grains such as barley and wheat should be avoided as they can induce colic.

SPECIAL FOODS

Chopped grass or lawn mowings: Although there is no doubt that cut green grass is as perfectly appropriate for ponies as if they had cropped it themselves, it must be fresh and fed in only small amounts. Once cut, grass soon starts to ferment and heat up, especially if it is very succulent and full of juice. In a pile, such heated grass rapidly decomposes and produces chemicals that can cause dangerous problems once inside your pet. Lawn mowings, being fine and tending to compress into a dense heap, ferment and heat more vigorously than grass cut with shears or a sickle and so present the greatest danger. If you feed mowings, do so very sparingly and only when just newly cut. If you have any doubts, DON'T give them, especially if chemicals, fertilizers, or weedkillers have

ABOVE: *This couple is obviously anxious to sample something other than grass.*

been used on the lawn. Lucerne (alfalfa) is an excellent, nutritious foodstuff but should be given in moderate amounts.

🔺 **Linseed:** This is another energy source and traditionally used to impart a sleek and glossy condition to the coat. On no account must it be fed raw—it can induce violent colic—nor should it be soaked in cold or tepid water to make a "mash" or it will release the highly poisonous chemical, prussic acid. Properly prepared by being boiled for three to four hours until it is a sticky gruel, allowed to cool and then fed, linseed mash is an excellent item on the winter menu.

🔺 **Invalid foods:** Gruels of oatmeal or barley meal are sometimes given to debilitated or convalescent animals. They are made by bringing 1 pound (450 g) of meal to the boil in

1 gallon (4 L) of water and simmering for 20–30 minutes. The cooked gruel is allowed to cool and fed, usually with the addition of some more cold water. Many people don't realize that both eggs and milk are suitable invalid foods for ponies. Milk can be given in quantities of up to 4–5 pints (2.5–3 L) a day and at first will be found more palatable by the patient if watered down and very highly salted. Eggs (two to six) are given raw, either beaten up in milk or mixed with a mash.

🔺 **Minerals and vitamins:** Although your pet should get enough minerals and vitamins from grass and/or the other ingredients of its balanced diet, it's wise to play safe, especially

RIGHT: *Every stable should be fitted out with a salt block.*

in winter. Add the recommended quantity of one of the equine mineral/vitamin supplements (some with protein added) that you can buy from pet stores, food merchants, and tack shops. These can be liquids, powders, or large blocks. Salt blocks are a sensible item in the stable, and glucose blocks can be given as a sort of lollipop treat in the winter.

AMOUNTS OF FOOD

The right amount of food for the pony varies, depending on the weight and size of the animal, the work it does, the season of the year, and the amount of grazing available. As with human beings, some ponies easily put on "spare tires," whereas others can gobble away and stay on the skinny side. Ponies at grass and doing a little light work need only a small

quantity of energy food—the bulk comes from the pasture—and in spring, when the grass is rich in protein, the protein content of the energy food can be reduced.

The same ponies when stabled must be given both the bulk food and a higher quantity of energy food. Some ponies become rather "fresh," belligerent, and unruly on too high a proportion of energy food and will need it cut back: too rich a fuel makes their engines roar, but then four-star gas isn't right for two-star engines! Others, the sluggish, dreamy types, may benefit from having it increased.

Sometimes, cutting the oats down to reduce combativeness is accompanied by a loss of weight. In this case, substitute linseed mash or flaked corn for the oats. Ponies that have a good temperament but tend to become fat should have their hay reduced.

It's all a question of adjusting the diet composition and amounts to the particular

WATER

Domesticated ponies must be provided with plenty of clean, fresh water. They will consume between 2–4 gallons (9.5–19 L) every day. If there is no constant supply, give the water in buckets before feeding, not after. A hot, bothered pony that has just returned from vigorous exercise should be rested and cooled and have the sweat removed before watering.

TYPICAL FEEDING PROGRAMS

Pony size	Routine	Summer diet	Winter diet
14.2 hands	Out at grass during the day. Stabled at night. Ridden every day plus schooling, shows, etc.	Grass during day. 1½ pounds (3 kg) of hay and 1½–2 pounds (3-4 kg) of pony nuts and a handful of carrots.	11-15 pounds (5-7 kg) of hay and 9-11 pounds (4-5 kg) of pony nuts and some carrots.
14.0 hands	Out at grass during the day all year. Stabled at night in winter. Ridden every day in summer, twice weekly in winter.	Grass during day and 4 pounds (2 kg) of pony nuts if necessary.	11-15 pounds (5-7 kg) of hay and 5-7 pounds (2.5-3.5 kg) of pony nuts and a handful of carrots.
13.0 hands	Out at grass all year. Ridden daily in summer but only on weekends in winter.	Grass only.	13 pounds (6 kg) of hay and 2-3 pounds (1-1.5 kg) of pony nuts and a handful of carrots.

requirements of your pet. It won't take you long to get the feel of it. Fiddling around with the diet and watching the effect won't do him a scrap of harm. Above is a table for feeding ponies of different sizes with varying routines in summer and winter to give you some general guidance in the early days of keeping your new pony.

If you decide to feed "complete" horse and pony cubes that contain a lot of fiber and don't need hay in addition, then follow the manufacturers' recommendations on the bag for daily quantities.

SPECIAL CONDITIONS

If a pony is kept outside throughout the winter, it is an excellent idea to give him warm feeds of linseed mash every other day during foul weather in addition to the regular diet. Ponies kept under these conditions are best provided with hay without limit.

If your pony is about to enter a period of increased activity (the summer season of shows, vacations, and so on), increase the energy food accordingly. If he is ill or lame and "off," reduce the energy food, give a little extra hay, and use some bran mash to keep the bowels in order.

Whenever you change the diet, do it gradually. Finally, the golden rule: Feed little and often. Four feeds a day are better than two, and two are better than one.

FOOD FOR HEALTH

Good feeding contributes much to good skin health. An occasional linseed mash will help to give the coat a sheen and, in dry-skinned individuals, an occasional helping of unsaturated fatty acid in powder form added to the food is very beneficial. This type of product can be obtained from a veterinarian, pet shop, or tack shop.

CHAPTER FOUR

HOUSING AND GENERAL CARE

Wherever your pony lives, its year-round accommodation will depend on several factors. The kind of pony he is, the climate in your area, the quantity and quality of grazing available, and what kind of shelter from the elements is in place must all be taken into consideration. You may choose to stable your pony indoors, to keep him out at grass, or to do a bit of both. You must decide which method suits you and, more importantly, the pony best.

AT GRASS

If you have a piece of land for your pet, it cannot be regarded as permanent grazing unless it's at least 2 acres (0.9 ha) in size—and by that I mean good green stuff, not a rocky desert or a converted bombsite! A good rule is to calculate a minimum of 2^1/$_2$ acres (1 ha) per pony, but even so, the land will need "resting" for a month or two each year and will need not only its own grooming in the form of attention to weeds, such as nettles, docks, and the dangerous ragwort, which can cause liver disease in equines, but also fertilization with lime or other chemicals, depending on the soil. After spraying weed killers and certain fertilizers, the animal must be kept off the ground for a period that can be as long as two or three weeks in the case of some brushwood killers (carefully read the instructions that come with the preparation you use).

It helps the land to graze more than one species together—for example, ponies with sheep and cattle. They reduce one another's parasites and one species trims back types of plants that the other ignores. Obviously, however, the more animals of any species, the more land they require.

If the pasture is large enough, try some form of rotational grazing, splitting it up with light fencing or electric fencing into zones that can be grazed and then rested in turn. Where you are really pushed for land, daily removal of the pony's droppings by a bucket and shovel will help to keep the grass clear and reduce the worm burden. Remember that some ponies tend to founder on fresh grass when it first comes in during spring.

BELOW: *This contented pair is grazing on obviously good-quality and abundant grass.*

FENCING AND GATES

This is expensive and you may have to put up with whatever comes with the land you rent or buy. Inspect your fencing regularly and keep it well maintained. At all costs, try to avoid barbed wire as a fencing material. It is vicious stuff!

ABOVE: *Protect young trees from ponies by erecting some protective fencing around them.*

ABOVE: *If you use electric fencing to split up a field for grazing, remember to clearly mark it.*

FIELD CHECKLIST

🔺 Is there enough space?

🔺 Is the pasture, the grass, of good quality? Avoid boggy, threadbare, very weedy, or too lush and rich fields. Check for the presence of poisonous plants (see page 59).

🔺 Is there a constant supply of clean, fresh water? Avoid or fence off muddy, slimy green (algae-covered) ponds. If there is no running water you will have to bring it in buckets or plastic drums at least once a day. Allow 9 gallons (40 L) per pony per day. Troughs must be cleaned regularly and should be free of sharp edges.

🔺 Is the fencing strong and in good condition?

🔺 Hedging or wooden post and rail are always preferable to barbed wire. Check the fencing regularly.

🔺 Is the gate strong, wide enough, and firmly hung? Can it be securely locked?

🔺 Is there shelter from driving rain, wind, and hot sunshine? This can be natural in the form of trees, hedges, walls, etc. or, best of all and if in doubt, a well-roofed shed placed on well-drained land, with its doorway facing away from the prevailing wind and a scattering of deep-litter (see page 62) dry straw bedding inside.

🔺 Is there company for the pony? If not other equines, perhaps sheep, cattle, goats?

🔺 Are there any hazards? Check for rubbish, broken glass, pieces of wire, and soon.

LEFT: *Strong three-bar fencing with the fence posts on the "outside" of the field is expensive but ideal. You must regularly maintain the fence, repairing any broken sections quickly and weather-proofing the wood.*

RIGHT: Temporary wire mesh fencing is cheap and easy to handle but dangerous to ponies that can easily break it down and trap their legs in the holes. If you must use it, for example, to keep grazing animals out of newly planted areas, create a barrier between it and your ponies with electric fencing that is suitably marked.

ABOVE: A strong wooden gate, with strong hinges, which opens into the field, is recommended. Heavy metal gates can rust easily, be difficult to open while handling ponies, and can trap a pony's hoof in the grid. Note the white electric strip along the fence to protect the saplings.

RIGHT: A metal sprung gate handle, which requires only one hand to open and close the gate, is ideal.

ABOVE: Remember to padlock a remote or isolated field to prevent other people from accidentally leaving the gate open and for your animal's security.

FIELD SHELTERS

Even if you have enough land to keep your pet outdoors, it still needs shelter from the elements, particularly in winter. An open shed or shelter, one that has the front partly closed, is essential. It should be big enough to give

ABOVE: *It is important to select the best position for a field shelter, preferably on dry, well-drained soil with the entrance facing away from prevailing winds.*

BELOW: *Field shelters are best constructed of creosoted wood, bricks, or breeze blocks. Corrugated iron is fine for roofs but best not used for walls. It is a*

WATER SUPPLY

Plastic trash pails make good water containers. They are not knocked over as easily as buckets and don't clip the pony's knees as old metal baths are prone to do.

poor insulator and easily works loose or curls at the edges. The result can be annoying rattling or, even worse, injuries to the animals.

Although many tough native ponies do not need blankets in winter, more delicate types and "senior citizens" appreciate the comfort of a New Zealand rug worn continuously in cold weather.

HOW TO TELL IF YOUR PONY IS COLD

If a pony feels cold, it may or may not shiver and it tends to be reluctant to move away from any available shelter. Place the flat of your hand on its skin over the chest and flanks; if the surface is uniformly cold it is best to warm the animal up right away by vigorous grooming ("strapping") or, particularly when wet, rubbing down with a twist of straw ("wisping"), bringing indoors to the shelter or stable, and/or blanketing it.

A sensitive pony exposed to much cold, particularly if wet as well, may develop respiratory problems.

one animal about 120 square feet (11 m2) with an extra 50 square feet (5 m2) for every additional animal. It need not be anything fancy so long as the roof does not leak and the walls are intact. The floor, which may be plain earth, must be dry and spread with straw in winter. The only essentials are a supply of fresh, clean water and some hay.

There is no need to remove soiled bedding from the shelter. Just regularly scatter clean new straw on top, thereby gradually building up a comfortable deep litter bed (see page 62).

Nor is there any need for a door on the shelter. Ponies prefer the entrance left open so they can see what's going on outside.

POISONOUS VEGETATION

Before putting a pony out to grass, or if you know the field where hay will be made for winter feeding for your animal, check for poisonous plants and don't forget to watch out for poisonous bushes and trees that may overhang from adjoining property. Some dangerous plants will be eaten by ponies only when other food is in short supply, or when they are dead and dried. Some have to be eaten regularly over weeks or months to cause their ill effects; others can kill after only a mouthful. Here are some of the most important toxic plants.

Yew *(Taxus spp.)*
Commonly found in English churchyards, this is deadly for equines. A handful can lead to fatal effects within minutes.

Bracken *(Pteridium aquilinum)*
Ponies usually like bracken only in late fall or when other grub is scarce. It contains a chemical that destroys vitamin B1. It usually has to be eaten over a period of months before producing symptoms.

Horsetail – also known as Marestail *(Equisetum spp.)*
Its effects are similar to those of bracken. It is usually eaten in hay.

Ragwort *(Senecio spp.)*
This causes liver damage after being consumed, usually in hay or when there is a shortage of other herbs, over weeks or months.
Note: Similar effects to Ragwort are produced by Rattleweed *(Crotalaria spp.)*, Peterson's Curse, or Salvation Jane *(Echium spp.)*, and Fiddleneck or Tarweed *(Amsinckia spp.)*.

Water Hemlock *(Cicuta spp.)* **and Hemlock** *(Conium maculatum)*
The symptoms of nervous system poisoning appear within two hours of ingestion.

Loco Weed *(Astragalus and Oxytropus spp.)*
Poisoning is most common in spring on the ranges in the western United States.

Sneezeweed *(Helenium spp.)*
A common poisonous weed of damp fields in the eastern United States. The flowers are the most toxic part of the plant.

Yellow Star Thistle *(Centaurea sostitialis)*
This is found mainly in the United States. It has to be ingested in large amounts over an extended period.

White Snakeroot *(Eupatorium rugosum)*
This is found in the southern United States. The poison attacks the nervous system and can kill an animal within days.

Milkweed *(Ascelpia spp.)*, **Rhododendron** *(Rhododendron spp.)*, **and Foxglove** *(Digitalis spp.)*
All contain chemicals that affect the heart and can cause sudden death.
Note: There are many other poisonous plants that less frequently cause trouble for ponies; if you are in doubt as to the identity and safety of any plant that might be nibbled by your pet, take a specimen to your veterinarian for identification.

SPRING GRASS

Many ponies are prone to founder on the lush, fresh grass when it first appears in spring. Ponies that tend to fatten easily need to be taken off this grass and either stabled or allowed to graze sparingly for only a few hours a day.

STABLING YOUR PONY

If you are stabling your pony indoors, you have the choice between a stalling system and a box stall. The latter is preferable as it allows more space and freedom to move around. It should provide the same area as mentioned earlier for sheds on pasture, and should be dry and well insulated. The floor should be nonslip (but not made of wood) and slightly sloping for easy drainage. It should be well ventilated and provided both with windows, barred on the inside, and with electric light. There should be a two-part door at least 4 feet (1.2 m) wide and opening outward. There should be no sharp projections, latches, or electric switches on the inside surfaces of the stable. If you use paint on the stable, never use lead-based paints.

MAINTENANCE

Somewhere near the box stall should be a separate room where all the mucking-out implements, food, bedding, and harness can be neatly stored. Food should be kept in galvanized, rodent-proof bins, and hay should also be held in well-built places where rat and mouse contamination is minimal. You will also need a suitable place for a muck-heap, and keeping a wheelbarrow.

Keep drains clear, walls, floors, and windows clean, and tack and food stores, as well as

BELOW: *The door is the right height for this pony, which will spend a lot of time looking out.*

BELOW: *A clean and tidy tack room is part of good pony-keeping practice.*

the stable, tidy at all times. You should keep your muck heap compact and tidy too—the more compact the muck is, the more it heats up and destroys worm eggs. To kill parasites in the cooler parts of the heap, turn them in with a fork occasionally.

You will also need clothing for your pet—a waterproof New Zealand rug, a stable blanket with a roller to keep it on, and some bandages to protect legs and tails. These are basic requirements; show ponies need extra, special equipment.

Finally, proper fire precautions should be observed. Extinguishers should be placed in readily accessible spots close to the stables and the hay and food stores.

EQUIPMENT

Only basic equipment should be fitted in the stable. This comprises:

- A ring for tying up to when necessary
- A manger or trough
- A water trough or bucket
- A hay rack (optional)

STABLE COMPANIONS

Ponies are best stabled with a companion— another pony or a donkey that they get along with or, if no other equine is available, a sheep or a goat will fit the bill.

BELOW: *Whether you use straw, wood shavings, or peat as bedding for your pony, you must always make sure that you have the correct facilities and equipment to correctly muck out the stable.*

MUCKING OUT

An essential daily job for the pony owner is mucking out the stable. An act of basic hygiene, it helps control the risk of certain ailments and it keeps the pony's living quarters dry and comfortable. Done correctly, using the right implements, it can take no more than a few minutes. And it is not really messy or smelly.

You will need a wheelbarrow, a shovel or long-handled scoop, a strong yard brush, and a stable pitchfork. It is best to turn the pony out and remove any portable water containers while mucking out.

1 Using the fork or shovel, put all manure and wet and dirty bedding into the wheelbarrow and take it to the muck heap, which should be situated well away from the stables.

2 Fork the rest of the bedding away from the center of the floor so that it lies against the walls of the stable.

3 Use a strong brush to sweep the floor so that it is ready for the new bedding.

DEEP LITTER SYSTEM

Alternatively, you can turn over the bedding by fork each day so that the droppings are buried. Very wet patches should be removed, and damp patches covered by dry bedding. A little clean bedding is now scattered all over. Gradually the layer of bedding builds up and its lower levels begin to produce heat by fermentation, killing parasites and other bugs, absorbing any dampness, and generally creating a warm, snug bed for the pony. Whereas traditional mucking out requires 3–6 bales of straw for one week, deep litter can be maintained on one or less. After some months, perhaps as long as a year, when it is becoming difficult for you to get into the stable, remove the bed and start again.

BEDDING DOWN

Stable bedding should be deep enough so that when a fork is stuck into it, the prongs do not touch the floor. Build up the bedding around the sides of the stable to keep out drafts, protect the pony from abrasions when lying down against a wall, and prevent it from becoming wedged when lying down and then unable to rise.

Some ponies love to eat their straw bedding and others are allergic to fungal spores in the straw that can cause coughing. For them, wood shavings, chopped hemp, dust-extracted straw, or shredded paper are better bedding materials, but these are all more expensive than straw.

1 Using a pitchfork or shovel, pile the straw up against a wall. Once a week disinfect the floor and leave it to air and dry for an hour or two before replacing the bedding.

2 Add new bedding, scattering it evenly in the center of the stable.

3 Bank the bedding up against the walls, making it deeper around the sides.

4 Let your pony back into the stable and keep an eye on him until you are happy.

STABLE ROUTINE

A pony is not usually kept in its stable night and day—unless the weather is particularly bad or the animal is not well, or there are other pressing reasons for doing so temporarily. Ponies thrive on space; they need to be able to stretch their legs, roll around when they feel inclined, and generally exercise themselves in the open air. A pony housed indoors permanently can become irritable, fractious, and prone to leg swelling and digestive upsets. In most cases stabling at night and putting the pony out during the day is a good routine to get into. At the very least, a stabled pony should always have two hours outside, either being ridden or wandering free in a field or paddock each day.

DAILY TIMETABLE

Assuming that you follow the "in stable by night—in field by day" routine for your pet, there should be at least four feeds per day provided. Unlike some other species, ponies have digestive systems that do not function well on just morning and evening feeds. An ideal daily timetable is the following:

Early morning:	Check the pony. Provide fresh water. Give first feed plus some hay.
Mid morning:	Muck out stable. Basic light grooming. Exercise for 1–2 hours.
Around midday:	Feed and give a full grooming. Provide more hay.
Afternoon:	Pony free to wander in field or paddock.
Early evening:	Feed, plus more hay. Put on night blanket. Check bedding.
Last thing:	Feed, plus more hay.

On any day when the pony has less than the usual amount of exercise, increase the amount of hay in the feeds and reduce the concentrates.

ABOVE: *Displaying obvious elation, ponies dash off when first turned out.*

GROOMING

The hairy coat of a pony is more than just an adornment and it does require regular attention and grooming from a thoughtful and proud owner. Obviously, wild ponies and asses don't get groomed—you would be lucky to get anywhere near them with a curry comb! But they do keep their coats in tip-top shape by mutual grooming and do-it-yourself mudpacks.

Wild ponies display elaborate grooming procedures that, apart from cleaning the coat, getting rid of parasites, and generally tidying up loose hairs, also act as vital bits of socializing that keep the members of the herd committed to one another. Flicking of the skin caused by rapid contractions of subcutaneous muscles, shaking the body, licking, and rubbing are all natural grooming movements. Scratching one hind leg against the other is never seen in wild ponies and horses but it is common among zebras.

Rolling in dust and mud is another favorite form of self-care for their upholstery, and experiments have shown that zebras will "recognize" and make overtures to a stuffed dummy zebra only if it is first properly smeared with a generous helping of glorious mud!

The most important and highly developed form of skin care in equines is biting. They bite themselves but prefer to do it to one another. One animal approaches its fellows and puts on the so-called "invitation face" (mouth closed and upper lip pulled forward). Without more ado they stand side by side, head to tail, nibbling away at one another's hide, rooting out old hairs, stimulating the blood flow, and toning up the bodywork. Each animal bites at

BELOW: *Ponies love being groomed—either by one another, OR BY YOU.*

the same area of skin as the other. This behavior is particularly important when winter coats begin to be shed and it is most prevalent during the summer. The molting of a pony's coat is stimulated by the spring rise in air temperatures. In the last wild horse, the Przewalski, which should strictly be called a pony, the temperature at which molting is triggered is 42°F (6°C).

This self-grooming in wild equines is all very well, but our domesticated friends need some regular and thorough help from their owner-drivers if they are to feel and look really good. Groom your pet properly and you will reduce the risk of skin disease, improve his condition, and make him elegantly glossy.

GROOMING YOUR PONY

Whereas the fond car owner appears on the driveway with hose and polish most Sunday mornings or, more lazily, takes his steed down to the car wash, pony owners must tend to the

appearance of their animals more regularly and frequently than that. Grooming is not a cosmetic procedure. Cleaning and brushing the coat has the following functions:

🐎 It reduces the risk of skin disease.

🐎 Very importantly, it pleases the animal and strengthens the bond between pony and rider.

🐎 It allows the groom to spot any minor cuts and injuries on the pony.

🐎 It stimulates the pony's circulation and muscle tone.

Ponies at grass in winter need little attention apart from a general looking-over once a week to remove any caked mud with a dandy brush, untangling of manes and tails, picking out and oiling of the hooves with neat's foot or some proprietary hoof dressing, and a general brushing down of the coat. In summer, grooming should be more thorough and frequent, and stabled animals also need more detailed daily attention.

LEFT: *This little character needs to have all the winter's mud brushed out of his coat.*

GROOMING EQUIPMENT

1 Slicker block: Good for removing winter coat and loose hairs and polishing the coat.

2 Rubber curry comb: A softer brush for deeper cleaning of the hairy coat.

3 Uni groom: Massager and winter coat remover.

4 Mane comb: For finishing.

5 Curry comb: Used as a body brush for cleaning the coat.

6 Grooming mitt: Excellent for removing the winter coat.

7 Cactus cloth mitt: For stains, sweat marks, and a final polish.

8 Comb: For combing the mane and tail.

9 Pulling comb: To tidy and shorten manes and strip out long hairs.

10 Hoof oil brush: For painting on hoof oil (dressing).

11 Hoof pick with brush: For picking out and brushing hooves.

12 Hoof pick: For picking out stones from hooves.

13 Sponges (2): One for the face and one for the rear of the pony.

14 Uni-groom: Good for massage, cleaning faces, and sweat marks.

15 Sweat scraper: Sweat and excess water remover.

16 Curry comb: For manes and tails.

17 Dandy brush: Used for the initial grooming brush.

18 Body brush: Good for removing dust and mites from the coat.

19 Water brush: For applying water and brushing a wet coat.

20 Hoof brush: Small brush to get into the hoof grooves.

21 Face brush: Small brush for those delicate areas around the eyes and mouth.

BASIC GROOMING ROUTINE FOR A STABLED PONY

When grooming your pony, always face the pony's quarters, never away from them. Nor should you stand directly behind him or you may receive a shove or a kick! It is best to groom outside the stable where it is less dusty.

TYING UP

1 Tie your pony up to a string loop through a metal ring, using a head harness and halter, and a quick-release safety knot.

2 Pass the rope through the string tie-ring and make a loop with the loose end. Thread through the first loop.

3 Tighten it by pulling on the half-bow but leave the loose end hanging down. You can release the horse quickly if necessary.

PRE-GROOMING CLEAN

1 Wash off any major dirt, mud, and stains with the water brush. Do not be rough.

2 Brush in firm strokes with the dandy brush to remove any remaining mud and crusted dirt.

3 Beginning at the neck and working downward, rub in circular motions with the rubber curry comb.

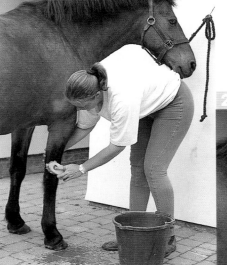

GROOMING THE MANE

1 With the mane comb and your fingers, gently untangle and comb through the mane, taking care not to pull the hair out.

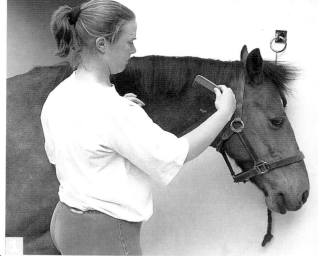

2 With the body brush, brush the mane over to the other side so that the brush goes right through the hair down to the roots where grease can accumulate.

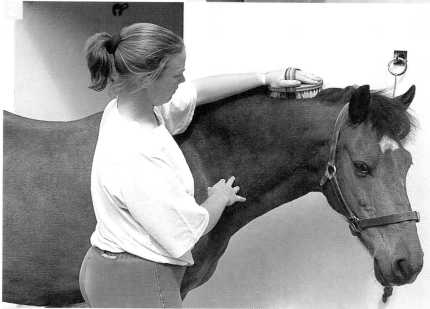

3 Brush the mane back over again to the original side, a little at a time. Afterward, brush and comb the tail.

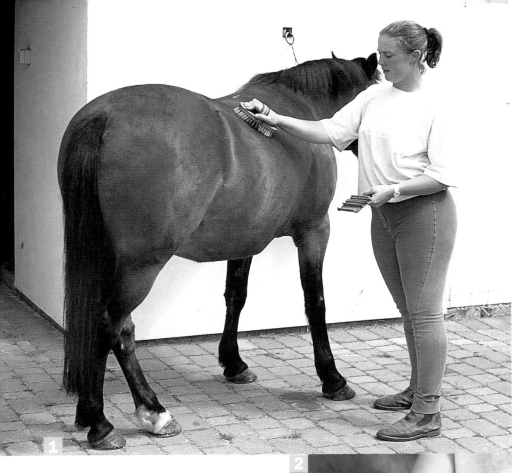

BODY BRUSH

1 Beginning at the top of the neck and working down, use the body brush, working in the direction of the hair.

2 After about a dozen strokes, scrape the brush on the teeth of a metal curry comb to clean out the bristles.

3 Alternatively, you can tap it against a wall or on the floor or, best of all, on a wooden board standing nearby.

SPONGING THE HEAD

1 Take the halter or head harness off the pony before brushing the head. If you wish, throw the lead rope around the horse's neck to retain control.

2 With the body brush, gently brush the head. Don't forget to brush under the jaw and the ears.

3 With a damp sponge, which is clean and soft and kept specifically for this purpose, sponge the eye area with clean, preferably warm, water. It should not be so wet that it gets water into the pony's eyes.

4 Rinse out the sponge and then sponge around the mouth and nostrils.

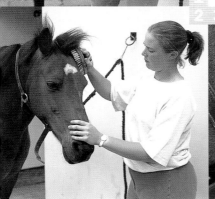

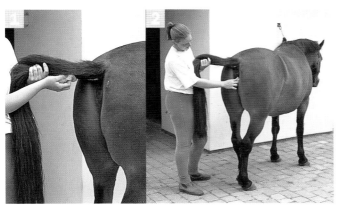

WASHING THE DOCK

1 With another damp sponge kept for this purpose, gently sponge the dock (the skin at the top of the pony's tail and above the anus).

2 Lift the tail while you sponge the area underneath. Take care not to mix up the sponges!

CHECKING THE HOOVES

1 Brush off the hoof walls, checking for any splitting.

2 Pick out the sole of the hoof. Remove foreign bodies and check the frog. Look for any soggy, smelly areas of rot.

3 Paint on hoof dressing to keep the wall strong and in good condition.

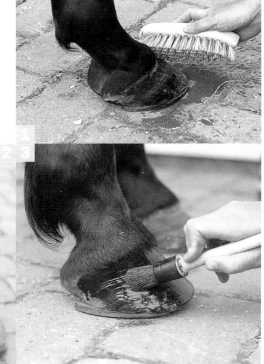

LAYING THE MANE

Using a damp water brush from which you have shaken out any excess water, brush the mane downward from the roots to the ends of the hairs. This makes the mane look neat and tidy with the hairs lying flat against the horse's head and neck.

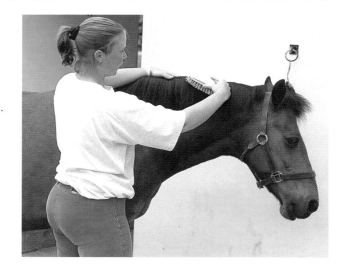

POLISHING

Finally, use the stable rubber all over the body to "polish" the coat and give it a healthy, glossy finish. Always wipe the pony's body in the direction in which the coat lies.

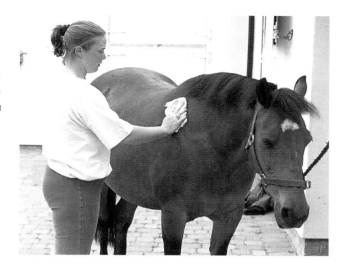

WASHING

Although very dirty areas, say the tail, can be washed off and dried during the winter, full bathing should be reserved for warmer weather. Even on the hottest summer day, always use at least lukewarm water.

🔺 Use a special horse shampoo.

🔺 Do not get shampoo into the pony's eyes.

🔺 Rinse and dry the pony thoroughly using towels.

🔺 Walk the pony around until it is completely dry.

🔺 Finish off by light grooming with a body brush.

🔺 If, by then, the air has grown cooler, put on a sweat blanket with a light sheet on top.

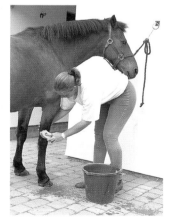

WASHING LEGS

There is much debate about washing ponies' legs as some animals on certain soils easily get inflamed, chafed skin around the pasterns ("mud fever") after a good day's trudging through the mire. In winter, ponies kept outdoors should have their legs washed only if they are badly clogged with mud. Don't clip any long hair off the back of the fetlocks. It is best to preserve the natural grease and hair protection of the coat during the bad weather. In summer, I prefer to wash off the legs if they are muddy and put stable bandages on the clean, wet legs overnight.

LEFT: *If your pony's legs are muddy in summer, you can wash them off with a brush and some lukewarm water.*

HOOF CARE

To examine a pony's hoof, you will need to pick up the foot. If you do this frequently, the pony will learn to lift the hoof for you, particularly if you always use a word such as "Lift" or "Foot" when you are doing it. For safety's sake, always approach the pony from the front, run your hands over him, and talk to him before checking the hooves.

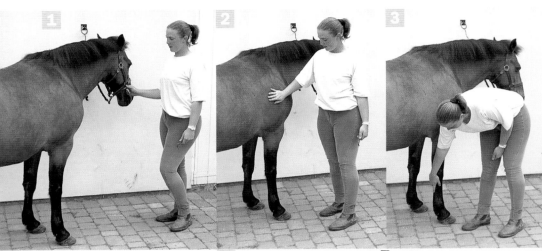

TO LIFT A FOREFOOT

1 Stand close to the animal facing its rear.

2 Run your hand down smoothly from the pony's shoulder to the fetlock.

3 Hold the fetlock firmly and bend it back.

4 Catch the front rim of the hoof with your other hand.

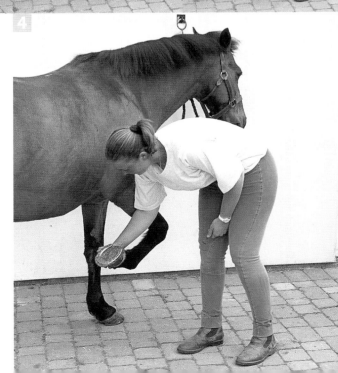

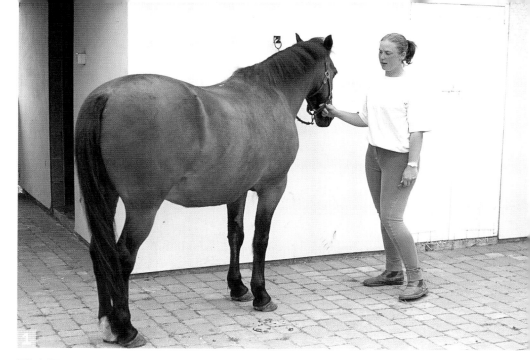

TO LIFT A HIND FOOT

1 Approach the pony from the head, standing close to it.

2 Run your hand along the pony's back as you approach its rear.

3 Stand close to the hindquarters, facing the rear of the pony and pressed against the hind leg so you cannot get kicked. Run your hand down the skin from buttock to fetlock and grab the joint firmly. Lift the fetlock forward and upward so all the leg joints bend. Take hold of the hoof rim and tuck yourself well into the pony's body.

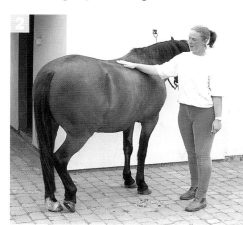

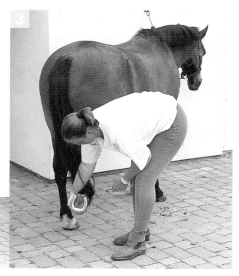

CHECKING THE CONDITION

Check the condition of the hooves regularly, looking for splits in the hoof wall, cleaning out dirt and stones from the grooves alongside the frog, and oiling the hoof as necessary. Do not use a hoof knife or penknife to pare away even flaking bits of the frog; you may inadvertently reduce frog pressure when the animal is walking or running. Frog pressure within the hoof is essential to good circulation and the health of the foot. Always leave frog trimming to the expert care of the blacksmith or veterinarian.

SPECIAL CARE

🔺 In winter, if the pony is going out into snow, apply a thick layer of grease to the soles of the hooves to prevent snow from compacting there.

ABOVE: *A liberal application of grease to the sole of the hoof is wise on snowy winter days.*

🔺 If a pony has hooves whose walls seem to be prone to dryness and splitting, then supplementing its food with biotin, a member of the vitamin B group, can help. Biotin powder can be obtained from feed merchants, veterinary pharmacists, and horse tack shops.

CHECKING THE SHOES

At your routine inspection of the pony's feet, keep an eye on the shoes. It is time to arrange an appointment with the blacksmith when:

🔺 A shoe has been lost, twisted, broken or is loose.

🔺 The shoes are worn thin.

🔺 The toes or heels of the hoof are beginning to overgrow the shoe.

🔺 The pony seems to stumble more often than before.

Note: You will need a farrier to trim the pony's hooves every two to three months, depending on how much it is ridden and how quickly the hoof wall grows.

UNSHOD PONIES

An unshod pony will still need regular attention from the blacksmith. The hoof is a living tissue that is constantly growing. As the hoof wall grows longer, it has a tendency to crack with potentially serious results. Skilled trimming is called for. Wild equines, of course, never see a blacksmith, but they keep their hooves naturally trimmed as they constantly move over rough or rocky ground.

LEFT: *Holding a foot up in the correct way to inspect the undersurface. This hoof belongs to a one-year-old unshod pony.*

CLOTHING

Some basic clothing should always be available for your pony. Seasonal and sudden weather changes, occasions when an animal is not well for some reason, or has been exerting itself—at times like these you may need to quickly dress the pony up.

SWEATING AND CHILLS

When a pony is sweating heavily in the stable after exercise, watch out for chills. Avoid these by rubbing the animal thoroughly with towels or wisps of hay, then sprinkle some straw on the animal's back and cover with a light blanket. After half an hour, remove the cover and towel or wisp again. A very hot and bothered pony should be walked around gently in the shade while covered with the straw and the blanket.

BELOW: *This pony's New Zealand rug is the correct size and is properly fitted.*

PROVIDING A BLANKET

A waterproof (New Zealand) rug should be provided for ponies wintered outside. However, several types of blankets are available and these are as follows:

New Zealand rug: This rug is the "overcoat" of the pony used to protect it against wind and rain. Although a tough little Dartmoor pony will thrive happily uncovered in all weather, it is best to put a blanket on the more delicate souls, the older ones, and any ponies that tend to be "rheumaticky"—just like humans!

Stable blanket: This one is put on indoors in chillier weather. It may be quilted or padded and is best fastened on the body with surcingles rather than the more uncomfortable and old-fashioned broad strap (roller).

Sweat blanket: The holes in the mesh trap

air that insulates the body. It is always used with a sheet (in warm weather) or a stable blanket (in cold weather) on top.

▲ **Exercise sheet:** Often waterproof, the exercise sheet covers the back beneath the saddle and can be used to keep the pony dry on winter rides.

▲ **Summer sheet:** The equine equivalent of the human beach shirt, this lightweight sheet is used in warm weather to keep flies off the pony and for traveling.

TOP RIGHT: *A summer sheet is lightweight and is usually made of cotton. It is used in summer when traveling or for keeping off flies.*
RIGHT: *A sweat blanket; the holes in the mesh trap air.*
BELOW: *As well as the heavy-duty blankets used for outdoor protection in winter, additional comfort can be provided by padded hoods.*

FITTING A STABLE BLANKET

A blanket should be the right size for your pony. It should fall on each side to cover the belly, elbows, and stifles and be long enough to cover the dock and buttocks. It should fit neatly over the shoulders, withers, ribs, and croup. To get an idea of the correct size before buying a blanket, measure the distance between the point of the breast and the point of the buttock.

1 Fold the blanket in half (with the inside out) and approach the pony from the front.

2 Put the folded blanket on the pony with its forward edge just in front of the withers.

3 Fold the blanket back, pulling it slightly toward the rear to neaten the fit, and then fasten the belly straps.

4 Carefully go behind the pony and fasten the hind leg straps.

5 Fasten the front straps, taking care not to pull the blanket forward over the pony's coat.

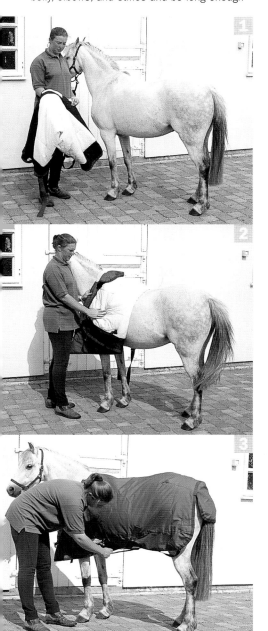

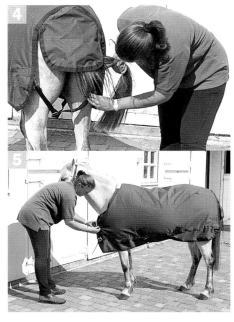

SADDLES

When obtaining a saddle, take advice from experienced people, preferably a master saddler. The saddle you choose will depend on your weight, your height, your pony's size and shape, and also what you want to do with your pony. Do you want to compete in Pony Club events, do jumping and dressage, or just have fun riding around?

Saddles must fit perfectly—at least as well as your own favorite comfortable shoes. Ill-fitting saddles can cause sores on the pony's back, which can become chronic and difficult to eradicate. The best saddles are English and they can be made to measure or ready-made. Measurements and fittings to ensure that you get the right size are always essential (see opposite). You may want a secondhand saddle; if so, fine, but inspect it carefully for undue wear, a broken internal framework, or flat, exhausted padding. An ill-fitting saddle will not only be painful for the pony but also will cause you to ride out of balance.

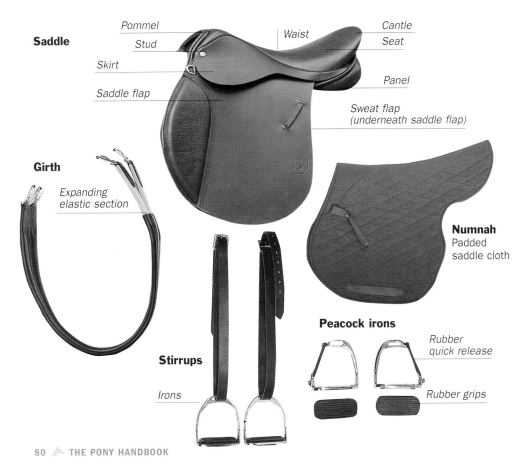

Saddle

Pommel
Stud
Skirt
Saddle flap

Waist
Cantle
Seat
Panel

Sweat flap
(underneath saddle flap)

Girth

Expanding
elastic section

Numnah
Padded
saddle cloth

Stirrups

Irons

Peacock irons

Rubber
quick release

Rubber grips

FITTING A SADDLE

It is essential for your pony's health and your safety as a rider that the saddle is fitted correctly by a qualified professional saddler. The saddle must distribute your weight properly and contour the pony so as not to inflict pain or discomfort.

LEFT: *The front arch of the saddle must conform to the pony's back for correct weight loading.*
1 The front arch is too narrow.
2 The front arch is too wide.
3 The front arch is the correct size for the pony.

LEFT: *The tree of the saddle (with the front arch) must conform exactly to the pony's shape as shown here.*

LEFT: *This saddle is too wide. If your weight is over the front arch, the saddle drops to find the wider part of the pony and the frame lifts off at the back, transferring weight to the front.*

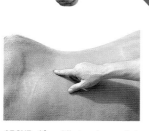

ABOVE: *After riding and removing the saddle, the hairs of the pony's coat should lie in a natural line.*

ABOVE: *This saddle is correctly fitted and will thus spread the rider's weight properly over the pony's body.*

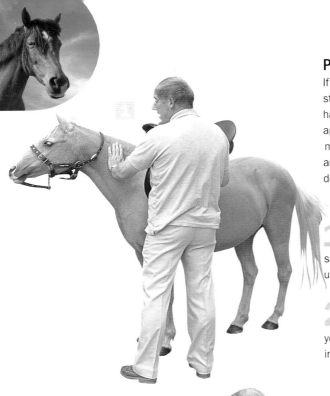

PUTTING ON A SADDLE

If you are not saddling up inside the stable, then either tie the pony up or have it held by someone else. Correct application and settling of the saddle is most important, not only for your comfort and security but to ensure that the pony doesn't develop saddle sores.

1 Approach the pony's near side, steadily talking gently to it. Hold the saddle with your right hand and forearm under the seat.

2 Place the saddle gently on the pony's withers, with the numnah beneath, if you are using one, and then slide it back into its correct position.

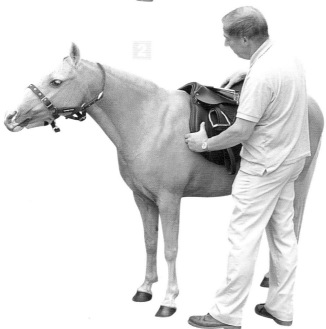

3 Go to the off side, let down the girth straps, and then return to the near side and take the straps from under the pony's belly.

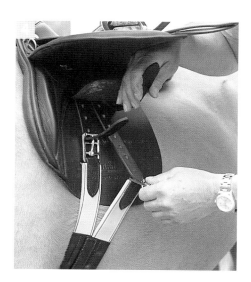

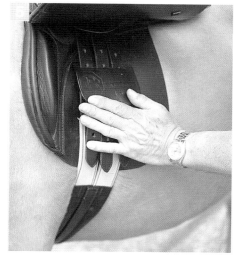

4 Do up the girth straps slowly, beginning with the front one and putting the strap through the top slot of the buckle. Don't tighten the straps excessively. Put a finger under each strap to check for wrinkled skin.

5 Fasten the back girth strap and adjust the buckle guard. Pull it down over the buckles.

6 Give the girth a final check to ensure that it is tightened correctly and make sure that no skin is wrinkled below before running down the stirrups.

7 This picture shows a correctly fitted saddle with the girth and stirrups in the correct position.

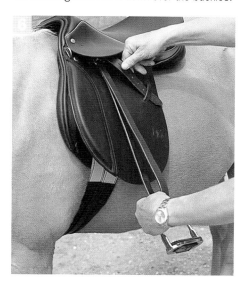

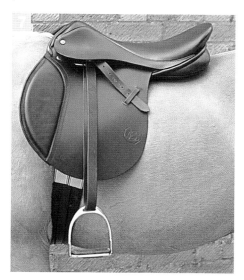

BRIDLES AND BITS

Controlling and steering the pony is done by specialized pieces of harness and equipment that link the rider's hands to the animal's head and particularly its mouth. The mouthpiece, or gag, comes in a multitude of designs, some of which are specially appropriate for certain types of riding or for specific types of pony.

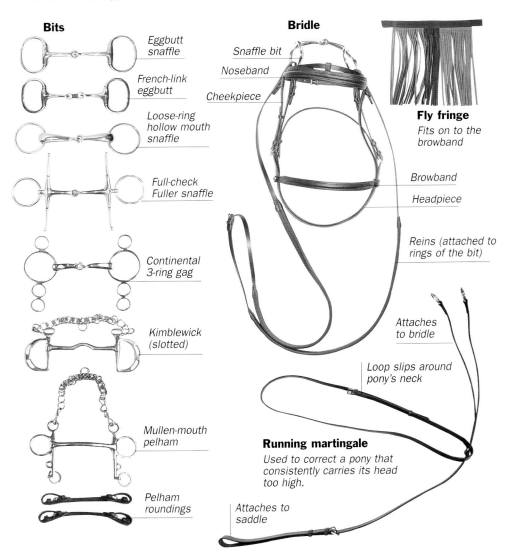

Bits

Eggbutt snaffle

French-link eggbutt

Loose-ring hollow mouth snaffle

Full-check Fuller snaffle

Continental 3-ring gag

Kimblewick (slotted)

Mullen-mouth pelham

Pelham roundings

Bridle

Snaffle bit

Noseband

Cheekpiece

Fly fringe
Fits on to the browband

Browband

Headpiece

Reins (attached to rings of the bit)

Attaches to bridle

Loop slips around pony's neck

Running martingale
Used to correct a pony that consistently carries its head too high.

Attaches to saddle

FITTING A BRIDLE

It is important for the pony's comfort and the rider's safety that the bridle fits correctly and is neither too big nor too small, too loose nor too tight. You can perform a few simple checks to ensure that this is the case. The best bit is the one that is kindest in allowing the pony to go forward under the correct control; the type used will depend on the pony's strength and temperament.

ABOVE: *Check that the cavesson isn't too tight. If you can't put a finger into the noseband, it may cut into the pony's nose.*

ABOVE: *Check the throat latch. You should be able to insert your hand sideways if it is fitted correctly.*

ABOVE: *Check the browband. You should be able to insert a finger between it and the pony's head.*

ABOVE: *There should be about $^1/_4$ inch (6 mm) between the side of the pony's mouth and the side of the bit.*

RIGHT: *The bit should always fit snugly in the pony's mouth.*

PUTTING ON A BRIDLE

The bridle, the contraption of leather straps that fits a pony's head, must fit properly and effectively and be kept in good condition for the animal's comfort and well-being and also for your safety. Always take advice from an experienced rider or professional saddler when first buying your pony's bridle.

1 Standing on the near side of the pony, slip the reins over its head.

2 Hold the bridle in front of the pony's face and then guide the bit very gently into the mouth.

3 Bring the headpiece up over one and then the other ear.

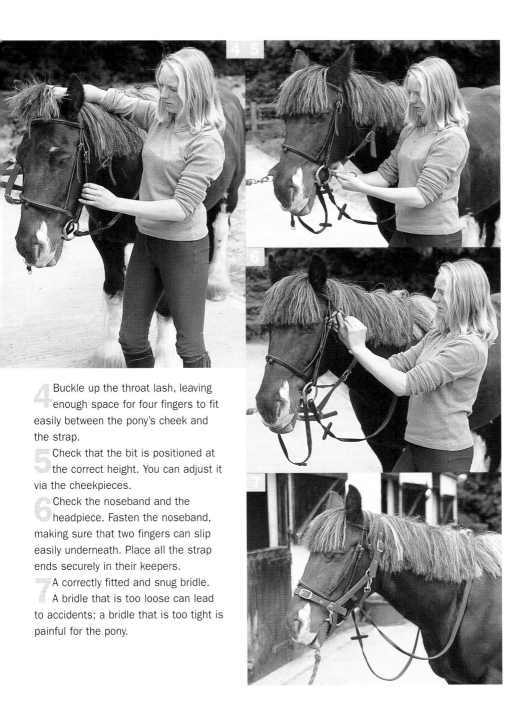

4 Buckle up the throat lash, leaving enough space for four fingers to fit easily between the pony's cheek and the strap.

5 Check that the bit is positioned at the correct height. You can adjust it via the cheekpieces.

6 Check the noseband and the headpiece. Fasten the noseband, making sure that two fingers can slip easily underneath. Place all the strap ends securely in their keepers.

7 A correctly fitted and snug bridle. A bridle that is too loose can lead to accidents; a bridle that is too tight is painful for the pony.

CHAPTER FIVE

HANDLING YOUR PONY

In many ways, the most important aspect of pony keeping is learning how to handle the animal with skill and consideration. A happy duo of pony and owner, who are at ease with one another, is created by the firm but gentle application of touch, sound, and sight—it's all about communication between you and the relationship that you build with one another.

APPROACHING YOUR PONY

Like many other animals, ponies are not very happy with unpredictable, erratic, excitable, or noisy human beings. Their sensitive, watchful natures, stemming from wild ancestors who had to be always ready to react instantaneously to prowling predators, make them nervous and resentful of loud people who rush around, lose their temper, are spiteful or impatient. It may well be that their highly developed sense of smell enables them to detect changes in the chemical makeup of our human body odor when we become irate, panicky, or stressed—scents that our weak human noses cannot pick up but that disturb their equine composure.

So in every aspect of pony handling, it is important to be calm, collected, predictable, and steady, just as you want your pony to be. The more you practice it and do it, the easier and simpler it becomes. Who knows, if you get really good, you might even become a horse or pony "whisperer!"

ON PUBLIC ROADS

Take maximum care at all times. Motor vehicles and their drivers can be big trouble for ponies. Sadly, not enough drivers reduce their speed when approaching horses or ponies.

The basic rules for road safety are:

Go on the same side as the traffic, on the grass strip if there is one.

It is best to walk or trot. Do not canter on tarmac. Do not trot downhill. Never gallop.

Go slowly at a walking pace around corners.

If in doubt, lead the pony with you between him and the traffic. Keep talking to him.

Stand well back from crossings when trains are due to pass. Ponies are usually frightened by the noisy locomotives and their cars.

Always make courteous gestures of warning or thanks toward drivers.

When approaching a pony, try to do so at an angle to the length of its body and not from behind or immediately in front—the animal's blind spots. Always speak to it as you approach steadily and then stroke or scratch it. Ponies soon recognize particular words, so you can issue commands such as "Walk on," "Back," and, when it is necessary to reprove it, "No." Always give praise when it is due, in a gentle tone of voice. A correcting "No" should be delivered firmly and sternly but without shouting. Be consistent at all times and your pony will soon learn the basics of good behavior.

Rewards in the form of sugar lumps and the like should not be dispensed incessantly but rather from time to time, particularly when the pony cooperates in some way, such as allowing itself to be caught in the field.

BELOW: Three firm friends return home. When handling ponies, always be sure to stay calm and relaxed.

NOW FOR SOME IMPORTANT DON'TS:

🔺 **Never hit or grab at your pony.**

🔺 **Never wrap a lead rope around your hand or wrist; if the pony made a dash, you could be pulled along and possibly severely injured.**

🔺 **When tying up a pony, never attach it to a moveable object such as a gate, never tie it so short it cannot freely move its head, and never leave it alone when tied up. Use a secure quick-release knot such as the "highwayman's hitch," attached to something like a loop of twine that will break if there is an emergency.**

🔺 **When offering a tidbit, do so with the palm of your hand held absolutely straight. Do not curl up your fingers—they may be mistaken for the goodies!**

PUTTING ON A HARNESS

It is easy to tell if there is a good rapport between pony and owner, especially when it is time for harnessing. This should not be a haphazard, unpredictable confrontation but a quick, quiet, controlled, and trouble-free coming together of good pals.

1 Approach the pony from an angle, calmly and quietly and talking gently, with the bridle hidden from the pony's view.

2 Pass the lead rope around its neck to keep control if necessary.

3 Bring the harness up to the face but not in a rush or jerkily.

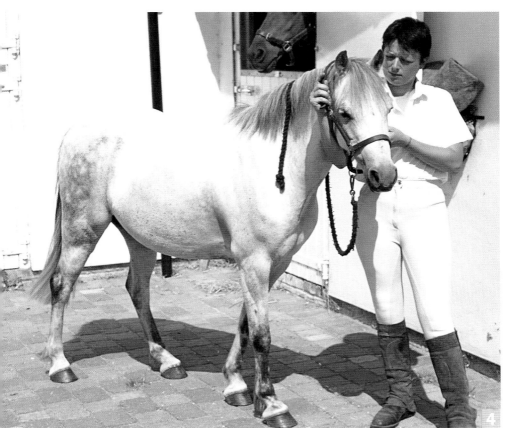

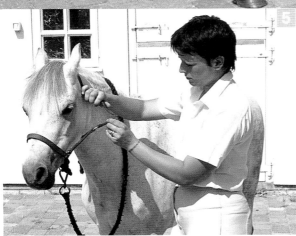

4 and **5** Do up the head strap and check that all the parts of the harness are properly seated and neither too tight nor too loose.

LEADING YOUR PONY

This is usually done from its left (near) side, although there is nothing wrong with leading on the right (off) side. With your right hand, hold the lead rope some 8–12 inches (20–30 cm) from the pony's muzzle, and carry the rest of the length of rope in your left hand.

▲ Always walk beside the pony, never behind or in front of it.

▲ Do not wrap the lead rope around your left hand or arm.

▲ Get your pony accustomed to being led from either its near or off side.

If leading your pony along a road, you should place yourself between it and the traffic (always walk on the side of the road with traffic).

ABOVE: *Normally a pony is led from its near (left) side, holding the lead rope or reins 8-12 inches (20-30 cm) from the animal's mouth in your right hand.*

ABOVE: *On roads, you should always place yourself between the pony and any traffic.*
RIGHT: *On roadways, ride in the same direction as the traffic. If possible, use the shoulder.*

TURNING A PONY

You will often have to turn a pony in one direction or the other, particularly if you are checking it over for soundness. As with everything to do with ponies, there is a right way and a wrong way of doing this.

1 When turning a pony, always hold it quite close to the mouth.

2 Always turn the pony away from you. You are likely to get stepped on if you try turning it toward you.

3 Don't forget to talk gently to the pony all the time while turning it.

ENTERING A FIELD

This apparently simple procedure must always be done correctly if all sorts of mishaps and accidents are to be avoided.

1 You walk slightly ahead of your pony, without letting go of him, in order to deal with the latch on the gate.

2 Open the gate wide enough for both of you and lead the pony through, holding him fairly close to the mouth.

3 Close the gate while still holding the pony with one hand. Walk into the field a few paces and turn the pony around to face the gate. Let him stand for a few moments, slip off the head collar, and let him go.

CATCHING A PONY

Like children who enjoy playing outdoors, most ponies sometimes prefer not to be caught. It's a beautiful day, the grazing is delicious at this time of year, and I'm enjoying being nibbled by my old pal, the donkey—so why should I go off who knows where with my owner?

Some ponies are always easy to catch, but others can pose more of a challenge. What should you do? Never try to chase or corner your pony. He'll enjoy the sport and he's nimbler than you. Be patient and have rewards in the form of sugar lumps, etc. Always praise and fuss over him when, eventually, you succeed.

1 Enter the field and approach the pony steadily, certainly not rushing, and at an angle to his shoulder, holding the head collar behind your back or close to your side.

2 Talking gently all the time, pass the lead rope around his neck and then slide on the head collar.

3 Adjust the head straps. (Ponies that are consistently hard to catch can be left out in the field wearing a leather head collar with about 12 inches [30 cm] of rope attached.)

> **WARNING:**
>
> **If you go to the field with the intention of catching your pony and tacking him up and you find him standing conveniently by the entrance, do not, in a fit of laziness, attempt to put on the bridle or head collar by simply leaning over the gate. That is the way accidents happen!**

CHAPTER SIX

HEALTHCARE

In general, ponies are hale and healthy animals, not prone to ailments. With good management and nutrition, they live longer and see less of the veterinarian than most other domesticated animals. When things do go wrong, they are frequently afflictions related to the special anatomy and physiology of the equine. The responsible owner must know what to watch out for and have a basic understanding of first aid, while never delaying unnecessarily getting professional help. The veterinarian is a vital friend in looking after your pony's well-being. Seek out one whose practice contains plenty of equine work rather than another whose patients are mostly small animals. Rely on veterinary advice when buying a new pony and see your veterinarian at least once a year for routine vaccinations.

HEALTHCARE

Just as you quickly realize that something is wrong when a friend or relative is feeling unwell, so it is with your pony. When you have known one another for a little while, you will have no difficulty in spotting that he is a bit out of sorts. Every time you go to your pony, take a few moments to check him over. Look at, listen to, and, of course, as you should do whenever approaching him, touch the animal. It is best to run through a routine of checkpoints every day. You will quickly learn to detect anything abnormal.

DAILY CHECKLIST

🔺 Stand back a bit and look at the pony overall. Is he alert and bright and glad to see you? Are his posture and general behavior normal?

🔺 Is the coat lying normally, dry and shiny and not "staring" or sweaty?

🔺 Is the pony eating and drinking his normal rations with gusto?

🔺 Listen carefully. Any dry cough or wheezing? Is his breathing normal?

🔺 Are the eyes and nostrils free of discharge? Are the membranes that line the eyelids, nostrils, and mouth moist and pale pink, not pallid, very red, or dry?

🔺 Watch the pony passing urine; is it clear, pale yellow, and voided without straining? Are the droppings of normal consistency—not too hard and not pasty or semiliquid?

🔺 Is your pony standing and walking normally? Check the legs for puffiness or the appearance of lumps and bumps. Is each fore- and hind leg symmetrical with its fellow on the opposite side?

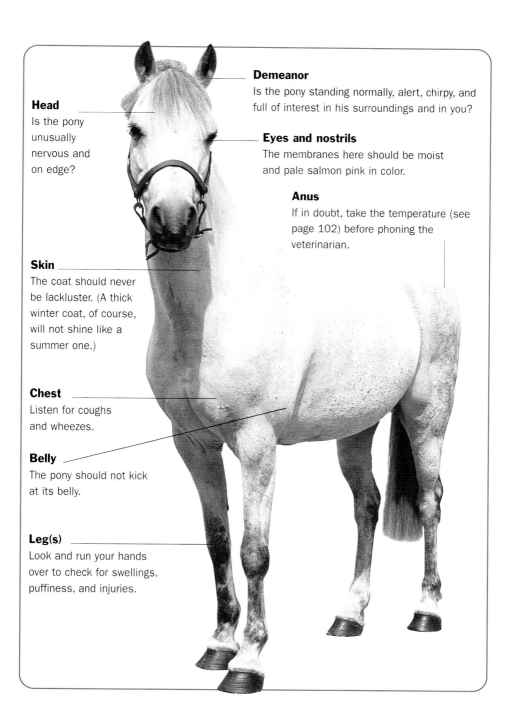

Head

Is the pony unusually nervous and on edge?

Demeanor

Is the pony standing normally, alert, chirpy, and full of interest in his surroundings and in you?

Eyes and nostrils

The membranes here should be moist and pale salmon pink in color.

Anus

If in doubt, take the temperature (see page 102) before phoning the veterinarian.

Skin

The coat should never be lackluster. (A thick winter coat, of course, will not shine like a summer one.)

Chest

Listen for coughs and wheezes.

Belly

The pony should not kick at its belly.

Leg(s)

Look and run your hands over to check for swellings, puffiness, and injuries.

GENERAL HEALTHCARE

TAKING THE TEMPERATURE

It isn't done by sticking a thermometer into your pony's mouth or under his foreleg. Put a halter or bridle on the animal and get someone to hold him. With one hand, hold the tail up as you stand close to the nearside (left) hind leg. Insert gently into the anus an ordinary clinical thermometer that has been greased with petroleum jelly or olive oil. When it is well in, angle it so that the bulb is pressed against one wall of the rectum.

TAKING THE PULSE

To find a pony's pulse rate, normally 35 to 40 beats per minute, place your first and second fingers under the back of the lower jawbone. With practice, you will feel the artery pulsating beneath the skin just on the inside of the jaw.

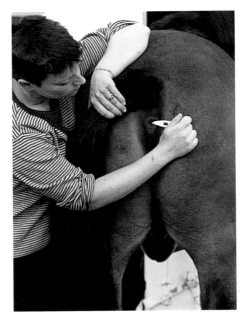

ABOVE: *To take the temperature, move aside the tail and gently insert a lubricated thermometer into the anus at an angle so that it presses against the rectal wall.*

The normal temperature of the pony is around 100.2°F (38°C), higher than humans but lower than that of other domestic animals.

EXAMINING THE MOUTH

To look in an equine mouth (to inspect the teeth, for example), have the animal haltered or bridled and preferably held by someone else. Standing on the nearside (left), push your hand between the lips behind the incisors. There is a large toothless space here. Grab hold of the slippery, sliding tongue—it is rather like grasping a wriggling eel. Gently but firmly pull the tongue out between the lips on the nearside and hold it. You can use the

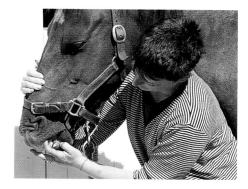

ABOVE: *A good position, gently restraining the head while examining the pony's mouth.*

tongue gently to "level" the mouth open, enabling you to look into its depths. A flashlight is often useful. Unless you are an expert, do not put your other hand into the space between the upper and lower molars—it is easy to have your fingers crushed painfully if your grip on the tongue slips, and sometimes even if it doesn't.

RESTRAINING YOUR PONY

Sometimes it is necessary to apply light restraint to an animal, when, for example, the veterinarian is giving an injection or examining the body. The way to do this is to lift a foreleg and stand holding it in a position close to the animal and facing its tail. The correct way to pick up and hold a hind leg for inspection or cleaning a hoof is shown on page 75.

Restraining an animal by twitches and other contrivances is outside the scope of this book. This should rarely be necessary and is the province of experts. Many of the ingenious methods of days gone by—hobbles, casting, roping, and gagging—are no longer necessary because of the new range of modern tranquilizers and sedatives available to the veterinarian.

ADMINISTERING MEDICINES

The veterinarian treats many horse ailments today by injection. Drugs to be given by mouth are often formulated in special tasteless or pleasant-tasting granules or powders that can be mixed with mashes—even so, ponies have a good sense of taste and can be very finicky and suspicious about "doctored" grub. Adding jam or molasses can mask an odd flavor in the food. Another ploy is to mix the drug with a few squares of melted chocolate. Then let the chocolate set again in the refrigerator and present the candy to your pet with an innocent look on your face!

Giving large pills by means of a balling-gun is rare nowadays and should be left to the experts.

Drenching (pouring liquids into the animal) is not as easy as it sounds and is best left to a veterinarian. In the hands of a novice, this procedure can drench a person or, worse, introduce liquid into the animal's windpipe with serious or even fatal consequences.

To carry out this procedure, the veterinarian will have the pony haltered with its head as high as possible and in a straight line with its body. Using a metal or leather-covered drenching bottle, he or she will push the neck of the bottle into the space between the incisor and cheek teeth and turn it toward the gullet while slowly pouring in liquid a little at a time to allow the animal time to swallow.

BANDAGING

Applying a stable bandage is a very simple procedure that is necessary when the pony's legs need some protection for any reason. Start with the bandage rolled with the tapes or fastening inside of the roll. Hold the end of the bandage against the leg with one hand and then go around and around with the other hand, overlapping each turn by two-thirds of the breadth of the bandage. Finally, tie the bandage around the legs with a neat, tight bow on the outside.

1 Always put a layer of padding under a bandage. Check that it fits well and lies smoothly before covering.

2 Have the bandage already rolled before you begin bandaging the legs.

3 Hold the end of the bandage with one hand and then slowly begin to unroll it around the leg, pressing firmly.

4 Each turn of the bandage should overlap the previous one by two-thirds.

5 It's best to start at the top of the padding. When you reach the bottom of it, you should go back up again.

6 Fasten the bandage firmly, but not too tightly, with tapes or Velcro. You should be able to slip a finger down inside the bandage.

Protective boots

Boots of various types are used to protect the pony's legs from damage. This can occur when jumping or when there is a tendency for one leg to brush against another ("brushing") or when "overreaching," the hind legs clipping the heels of the forefeet when in motion.

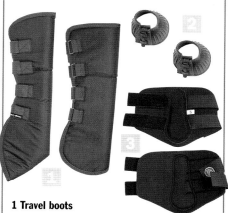

LEG PROTECTION

1 Travel boots
These cushion the legs from knocks and grazes while the pony is being transported in a vehicle.

2 Overreach boots
Used on the forefeet only to protect them from damage by overenthusiastic hind feet.

3 Brushing boots
Used when the pony is being ridden, particularly cross-country, to protect one leg from coming into contact with its fellow on the opposite side.

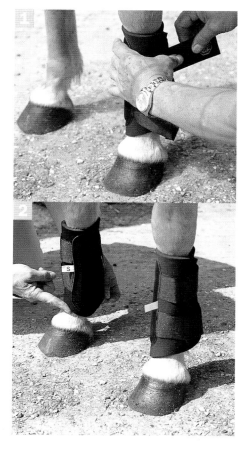

1 As with bandages, boots should fit snugly but not too tightly. You should be able to slip a finger down inside them.

2 Always fasten the straps of the boot on the outside of the leg.

GENERAL HANDLING

Whenever you examine your pony, stand close to it. The closer you are to the hind leg, pressing on it, the less risk you run of being on the receiving end of a kick that has some impetus behind it. Accustom the pony to being touched. Run your hands firmly over its head, neck, body, and, very important, legs regularly and frequently. Apart from accustoming the animal to your touch, this will also enable you to detect any abnormal "feel" under your hands in its earliest stages.

MEDICAL PROBLEMS

It is not my intention in this little book even to attempt a manual on the diagnosis and treatment of equine ailments by the lay owner. The modern medical approach to sick ponies is a complex professional task that should be left to the veterinarian. The days of "cure-all" bottles of physic, bloodletting, and mustard plasters have been left far behind and it is unfair to the animal, inefficient, and often dangerous and downright illegal for unqualified people who "reckon to know a bit about 'osses" to be allowed to play doctor with such precious creatures. The owner's responsibility is to be alert for signs of trouble, to supply good nursing and supportive treatment when the veterinarian has examined the pet, and to prevent problems, rather than cure them, through good stockmanship.

Ponies have some advantages and a few disadvantages compared to horses when it comes to health. Ponies are generally hardy and trouble-free but are particularly prone to recurrent bouts of laminitis. They never develop roaring or whistling, the windpipe troubles of their bigger relatives. And they tend, on average, to live longer than horses.

SIGNS OF ILLNESS

You will have come to know the personality and temperament of your pet, his attitudes, and his general approach to life. The first signs of trouble are ones that you will detect—alterations in the routine, the normal. There may be a change of mood to dullness or crankiness, a vague sluggishness, or a curious "something" in the way he moves. More obvious symptoms will relate to one of the major organ systems of his body, such as changes in the appearance of his droppings, slowness of eating or lack of appetite, change in the rhythm of his breathing and its intensity, discharges at one of the orifices of his body, or the development of troublesome areas on his skin or in the eyes. Many diseases of the horse affect more than one system in the body and diagnosis generally needs professional techniques.

TOOTH PROBLEMS

Your pony will rarely need dental treatment, although decayed teeth, root infections, and the like do occur. The most common fault is that the cheek teeth either develop sharp points or become worn down until their grinding surfaces are smooth. These alterations to the tooth profile can cause discomfort or simply difficulty in chewing food. They are seen most often in old animals but also occur from time to time in youngsters. The signs are slowness in eating and a tendency to sloppiness, with the dropping of food, particularly hay. The veterinarian can quite easily file off points or roughen smooth-surfaced teeth with a tooth file. It is a simple, painless procedure that may have to be repeated every three or four months.

EYE PROBLEMS

There are many different eye ailments. The most common are inflammation of the cornea and conjuctiva caused by injuries, by foreign bodies, such as grit or hay awns, or by a

ABOVE AND RIGHT: *To bathe a pony's eye, use warm water containing a little boric acid powder, and cotton. BE GENTLE.*

straightforward bacterial infection. Watch out for any discharge or excessive water from the eye or eyes, redness of the white of the eye, and any bluish haziness of the normally transparent cornea. At the first sign of any such abnormality, call the veterinarian and meanwhile bathe the eye gently with a warm (body heat) solution of one teaspoonful of boric acid dissolved in a cup of water. Don't

BELOW: *In summer, you can carefully apply some fly-repellent cream close to BUT NOT IN the eye.*

let matter build up around the eyelashes and on the lids as it will only make things worse. If flies are paying a lot of attention to sore eyes, ask your veterinarian for advice. If the eye is very sore and watering profusely, the animal would be best in a shady box stall until treatment begins to take effect.

CHEST PROBLEMS

Respiratory disease is common in equines. Signs may include one or more of the following:

- Nasal discharge
- Coughing
- Dullness
- Sweating
- Fever
- Fast or heavy breathing

There are several different types of chest problems, each with its own causes and symptoms, so early diagnosis is essential for correct treatment and proper recovery. Your job is to move the sick animal to a dry, warm, but well-ventilated, dust-free stable. No work should be done and it is often best to keep the animal lightly blanketed. A bran mash each day helps keep the bowels open. Provide easily digested food, soft new hay, and plenty of lukewarm water. Don't waste time administering cough medicines or other potions before calling the veterinarian.

Equine influenza and bacterial infections

Several viruses can produce chest ailments in equines; the most familiar is equine influenza. The virus attacks ponies and donkeys as well as horses but it can be guarded against by preventive vaccination. Initially two doses are given three to six weeks apart with a third dose five months later and annual boosters thereafter. Some makes of vaccines are administered at somewhat different intervals. The bacterial infections of the chest are treated by the veterinarian using injectable antibiotics and other drugs such as mucus liquifiers. Antibiotics are rarely given by mouth to equines, so as not to disturb the friendly digestive bacteria in the intestines, but sulphonamides and similar chemicals can be administered as powders mixed with food or as an oral paste in special syrups.

Broken wind

Cases of so-called "broken wind" in equines are the chronic result of dust from moldy hay or straw. There is no true cure, and prevention is the watchword—don't buy poor, damaged hay or straw, make sure stables are well ventilated, and don't store fodder above or very close to the animal's living quarters.

Lungworms

These are a particular risk in donkeys and can easily spread from them to their pony or horse stable companions. Newly arrived donkeys should be wormed before coming into contact with other equines, and all donkeys, ponies, and horses on the premises should be wormed regularly together at intervals of, say, three months.

GASTROINTESTINAL PROBLEMS

Colic

The most famous illness of horses, this is actually acute indigestion and comes in several forms, some mild, some serious and violent. The causes of colic are related to the management of the diet: Overfeeding, abrupt changes of diet, and unsuitable foodstuffs, such as wheat, moldy food, too much water given to a hot and tired animal, watering after a feed, and worms are the most common causes.

🔺 **Symptoms** A pony with colic shows these symptoms of abdominal pain:

🔺 It stops feeding.

🔺 It looks around at its flanks.

🔺 It kicks at its belly.

🔺 It lies down restlessly, soon to stand up and then just as soon lie down again, unable to find ease or comfort.

🔺 It may stand with hind legs apart as if trying to pass urine and, in severe cases where the pain is intense, may throw itself around alarmingly.

The pain is caused by spasms in the intestine walls and the presence of gas that disturbs the bowels. Few or no droppings are passed. If the bowel spasms are so intense that the intestinal wall twists or telescopes, cutting off its blood supply, the outcome is frequently fatal. Quick veterinary treatment, however, usually results in a complete recovery.

🔺 **Treatment** Your job is to send for the veterinarian and then try to relieve the

animal's discomfort as much as possible. Keep it warm by light blanketing and walk it around, preferably indoors if possible. Spread plenty of thick bedding around in case the animal goes down. Try to keep the animal as

ABOVE: *A lightly blanketed pony is walked around while waiting for the veterinarian to arrive.*

calm and as comfortable as possible until professional help arrives.

Note: You will notice that I do not mention vomiting as a symptom of colic (or any other tummy trouble in equines). The reason is that horses, ponies, and donkeys cannot vomit.

Diarrhea

This is very uncommon in ponies. It can be caused by infections, sudden alterations in the diet, poisons such as acorns (when taken in large amounts), insecticides, moldy food, or, most important of all, particularly in the young animal, worms. The condition always requires quick professional attention. Until the veterinarian arrives, keep the animal indoors and warm. Chcek with him or her before giving any food or drink to your pony.

WORMS

The horse family suffers from the attentions of many types of worms. Of the three main groups, roundworms (including lungworms), tapeworms, and flukeworms, it is usually the roundworm that causes all the trouble and sometimes death in horses, ponies, and donkeys. The worms live not just in the bowels but also in other places, such as lungs, tendons, skin, and even inside the eye. Intestinal worms spend part of their life cycle migrating through the body via the bloodstream, and the effects of their wanderings on the blood vessels can be severe and sometimes suddenly fatal.

Equines have their own particular worms, as do dogs, cats, sheep, and cattle. These worms are not interchangeable between species.

Although the large white roundworms, which can be 12 inches (30 cm) long and 1/4 inch (6 mm) thick and are a particular threat to foals, are easily seen in the droppings, other worm species are even more dangerous and not as easily visible.

▲ **Prevention** Ponies should receive regular worming medicine at least once every three months. There are various effective wormers available from the veterinarian, tack shop, or pharmacy. The modern ones, such as Ivermectin, will kill all the major species of dangerous worms. Worming medicine can be given as a powder mixed with the feed or as a paste squirted onto the tongue from a handy disposable oral doser. In order to avoid the worms developing resistance to your worming drug, it is a good idea to change the type of medicine from time to time. Check with your veterinarian.

BELOW: *One common way of worming a pony is by using a special worming syringe whose contents are squirted into the animal's mouth.*

TETANUS

Tetanus is a very serious disease that sometimes occurs in humans and other domestic and wild animals, but is a particular threat to equines. The germ enters the body through a wound, usually a badly aerated, soil-contaminated puncture, although it may also gain access to apparently uninjured animals, probably from the bowel via abrasions or ulcerations of the intestinal wall.

▲ **Symptoms** These are of progressive stiffness due to spasm of the body muscles.
▲ The limbs become rigid and somewhat splayed, like the legs of an old-fashioned milking stool.
▲ The tail becomes raised and the third eyelid moves over the eyeball.
▲ Increasing difficulty in opening the mouth due to the spasm of the jaw muscles gives the common name of the disease—lockjaw.
▲ Bright lights and noise increase the involuntary movement of the muscles.

▲ **Treatment** With vigorous treatment and careful nursing, about a half of tetanus cases can be expected to recover. The veterinarian will tackle the disease by trying to locate and disinfect the site of entry of the bacteria, and by administering antibiotics, tetanus antiserum, and special muscle-relaxant drugs. The owner has much to do, nursing the animal in quiet, dimly lit quarters, giving nourishment by any route possible, and even supporting the patient in slings.

▲ **Prevention** Your chief responsibility is to prevent the risk of tetanus in your pet. Make sure it is vaccinated against the disease and that it receives yearly booster injections. Unvaccinated animals that are wounded need

VACCINATIONS

Every pony should be vaccinated against tetanus (see left) and equine influenza (see page 108), most particularly if you hear of an outbreak in your area. The vaccines can be administered to healthy animals by the veterinarian in most cases from the age of three to four months.

The timing of when best to first vaccinate a young pony will depend on a number of factors, such as the degree to which a young foal derives some immunity in the form of antibodies against a disease from its mother; your veterinarian will advise you about this. Combined tetanus/influenza vaccines are now available.

You must remember to follow up the initial vaccination course with annual booster shots that maintain the protection. Other vaccines that are used under special circumstances are those against equine herpes viruses that can cause another variety of respiratory disease and rabies. Your veterinarian will advise you should they be deemed necessary. Rabies shots, for example, would be wise if you are taking your pony to areas where rabies exists in wildlife.

There are other, less common complaints against which a pony can be protected by vaccination. Whatever you do, when you first acquire a pony, DISCUSS WITH YOUR VETERINARIAN IMMUNIZATION THAT IS APPROPRIATE TO THE AREA IN WHICH YOU LIVE.

the immediate but short-term protection of an injection of tetanus antiserum, together with the first dose of tetanus vaccine to begin long-term immunity.

SKIN DISEASES

There are many kinds of skin diseases in equines, and abnormal changes in the texture and appearance of the skin can result from the invasion of microbes, parasites of many different species, foreign bodies, allergies, sensitivity to light induced by eating certain plants, warts and other growths, dietary factors, and other things.

Parasites

If you see parasites, such as lice, ticks, or (rarely) fleas, on your pet, dusting him with some medicated powder or shampooing with an appropriate horse shampoo, both obtainable from a veterinary supply catalog or tack shop, will eradicate the problem. Other types of skin ailments need professional diagnosis.

Saddle sores

A fair number of sores in the saddle region are caused, particularly in riding ponies, by ill-fitting tack. You must buy the best tack you can afford and have it fitted to your pony by an experienced saddler. It must be properly cleaned and maintained and stored in a dry, clean, orderly place. Buying tack "off the rack" without trying it for size, fit, and comfort on the animal is like buying false teeth by mail order.

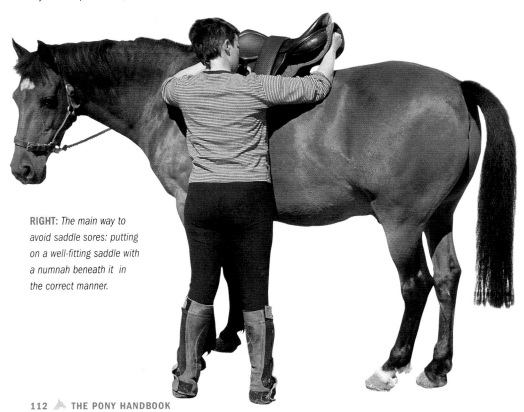

RIGHT: *The main way to avoid saddle sores: putting on a well-fitting saddle with a numnah beneath it in the correct manner.*

LAMENESS

Horses and ponies evolved their extraordinary limbs to enable them to speed away from danger. In doing so, they modified their legs and feet so that they now walk and run on the equivalent of one toe (or finger) on each leg, the nail having been enlarged into a hoof. A side effect of this development has been a susceptibility to lameness; everything depends on the simple "toe" and it can easily be damaged or develop problems.

Lameness is common in ponies and it can strike without warning. It is no respecter of equine persons, and is as likely to lay low a racing thoroughbred as any long-suffering pony. It may be caused by a number of factors, including wounds; bruising; damage to muscles, nerves, tendons, ligaments, or bones; dislocations; arthritis-type conditions (splints, ringbones, and navicular disease); inflammation of the bags of lubricating liquid that protect a joint or tendon (windgall, capped hocks, and bog spavins); a disease of the foot (laminitis and canker); damage to the hoof wall; shoeing faults; skin disease (grease and mud fever); and bone disease (rickets).

The affected area can be in the groin, back muscles, legs, or feet. The causes of lameness vary widely and the diagnosis and treatment may be relatively simple or extremely difficult. Early treatment is essential to prevent acute conditions (those that come on suddenly and don't last long) from becoming chronic (long-term and well established).

▲ **Treatment** The veterinary treatment of lameness depends on the nature of the problem, ranging from drug therapy to surgical methods of repairing damaged tissues or removing diseased areas. However, sometimes the cooperation and skill of the local blacksmith is called for in order to relieve certain lameness in ponies by the fitting of special "surgical" shoes.

▲ **Prevention** Your job is to watch out for any signs of lameness in your pony and to act promptly, and also to ensure that your animal's legs and feet are always kept in good condition. Regular examination of the limbs and feet, coupled with attention from time to time by the blacksmith, who will tidy up hooves that are tending to overgrow and will fit good shoes to ponies at appropriate intervals, are essential preventive measures in avoiding this common health problem.

ACUTE LAMENESS

In cases of acute lameness where you can locate the site, your action should be:

1 Rest the animal indoors.

2 Bathe the affected part in cold water, hose with cold water, or apply ice bags.

3 If the lameness is in a limb, apply one of the special dressings, available from the tack shop or pharmacy, or wrap it in cloths soaked in a cooled infusion of comfrey leaves.

Note: Don't start rubbing on liniments or other potions or administering medicines that were perhaps left over from other cases of lameness. Call the veterinarian for professional advice and treatment.

LAMENESS—TELLTALE SIGNS

I am not expecting you to be an expert diagnostician of the origins of lameness. However, there are some important telltale signs that you must be on the watch for.

🔺 At the first sign of abnormal action or movement, try to locate which part of the body or limb is affected.

🔺 If an animal is lame in the foreleg, watch it from in front: It will nod its head downward as the good foreleg strikes the ground.

🔺 If a hind leg is in trouble, view from behind; The point of the hock of the good leg travels a greater distance up and down than the point of the hock on the bad leg.

Of course, these are the simplest cases. If the trouble is in the back, the pelvis, or in more than one leg at the same time, things can be more difficult to identify. Don't try to guess.

🔺 You can run your hand over the body and particularly the limbs, looking for tender spots or unusual swellings.

🔺 You can inspect carefully for wounds, for signs of disease on the surface, and for areas that are unusually hot, as compared perhaps with the corresponding parts on the opposite side of the pony's body.

🔺 Check the hoof for picked-up stones and for signs of injury or disease on the sole or frog.

ABOVE: *Watching the pony's action when it is moving on a hard surface with someone else leading it is the best way to check for signs of lameness.*

PONIES AND LAMINITIS

Laminitis is a common complaint of ponies, particularly in the spring and in overfed little fatties! It can also be induced by some form of indigestion, a sudden change of diet, or food that is "off" in some way, or in animals with a feverish disease such as pneumonia, inflammation of the uterus, or retention of the afterbirth after foaling. The disease is an inflammation of the horn-producing tissues below the hoof and it occurs normally in all four or at least two feet. It is very painful and the animal stands miserably, often with the forefeet as far forward as possible and the hind feet pulled well under the body. It literally hasn't got a foot to stand on—all are equally punishing—and it doesn't like the feet to be handled or picked up. The temperature is often raised by two to four degrees.

BELOW: *Keep the sick pony warm with plenty of soft bedding and even a light blanket if required.*

Treatment Laminitis cases need veterinary treatment and modern drugs in order to relieve the pain and suppress the inflammation. Your job is to rest the animal indoors on lots of thick, soft bedding or, if available, damp clay. Keep the animal warm, if necessary with a light blanket, and encourage it to drink plenty of water. A bran mash to keep the bowels open should be given each day.

Prevention Ponies on rich pasture in spring or ones that are spoiled with constant overedfeeding may have recurrent attacks of laminitis that gradually deform the feet; they become "slipper-shaped," with long, concave hoof walls that are grooved with distinct horizontal rings. At this stage veterinary treatment can only compensate for the altered action of the damaged feet by surgical shoeing and by regular attention from the blacksmith, who will attempt to bring the foot back little by

little toward its normal shape by cutting back the toe and shaving the hoof walls at the sides and heels to encourage contact of the frog with the ground and therefore better circulation of the blood in the foot.

It is your responsibility to avoid overfeeding, particularly in the spring, and to exercise your pony. You may have to slim down your pony by reducing drastically the amount of concentrates in its diet or even, if it is feeding purely on lush spring grass, allowing it only a couple of hours grazing per day, the rest of the time being spent in the stable or out exercising. However, all this is easier said than done. Owners find it very difficult to be tough with their pets but it really is in everybody's best interests—it can save your animal a great deal of suffering and a shortened life.

BELOW: *Too much lush new spring grass can cause problems with ponies' health and general well-being. Limit the amount of time they spend in the field.*

BREEDING

This book is not for those who want to go into the world of thoroughbred breeding with all the attendant mumbo jumbo, advanced science, and multitude of problems. Ponies left to their own devices and running wild have less trouble in reproducing their kind than do any pampered thoroughbreds. They find it no bother at all to have 95 percent of their mares conceiving and nearly that percentage giving birth to live foals without the need for human assistance or interference. The pony lover who wants a foal around the place won't find it quite as easy as wild pony herds, but it is still a fairly simple business with a success rate that, on average, produces one young, survivable foal every two years.

PREGNANCY

A horse's gestation period is eleven months. Mating occurs when the mare is in season (estrus) and will accept the male. Estrus occurs at intervals of three weeks between March and September and lasts for four to eight days. The longest pregnancy period of all equines is that of the Grevy's zebra—about 390 days!

Signs of a mare in season

What starts all this off is the increasing hours of daylight in spring. The light affects the eyes, which send a message to the brain that notifies the pituitary gland below the brain. The pituitary gland then sends a chemical hormone through the blood to the ovary and tells it to get busy gathering up egg cells.

When a mare enters estrus she becomes "different." She may seem more excitable

than usual or more placid. She stands from time to time with hind legs apart as if wanting to pass urine. The tail is raised and the lips of the vagina wink open and closed. She squeaks, fidgets, kicks, and squirts small amounts of urine if touched on the back or flanks. These symptoms are more exaggerated if a male is around, even though she may reject him and kick him in the first few days of heat. Later she is more compliant and allows mating. The best time to conceive is two days before the end of estrus but, as you don't know in advance when it will end, you should if possible allow mating to occur every other day while the mare will accept the male.

Young males are fertile by the time they are two years old and females can conceive at one year of age, though this is not a good idea; it is best to wait until females are at least two before mating. One of the most fertile heat periods is the so-called "foaling heat," which happens about one week after the mare gives birth. Statistically, more mares lose foals conceived at this time, and some veterinarians have reservations about the practice, but you can use this heat if you are

---

PONY CUSTOMS

In olden days, to find out whether a mare was pregnant or not, her owner would spit a mouthful of water into her ear. It was believed that if she was in foal she would shake only her head; if not, her whole body.

intent on repeat breeding.

If your mare doesn't come into heat and you really want a foal, consult your veterinarian. There are many causes of infertility and, after a thorough examination, he or she may prescribe hormone or other forms of therapy.

Pregnancy detection

From three weeks after mating, the veterinarian may often be able to do a manual inspection via the rectum if the mare is big enough. A blood test can be done by the veterinarian between 45 and 90 days into the suspected pregnancy. A urine test can be carried out after the 150th day.

THE BIRTH

The udder enlarges in the last months of pregnancy and a waxy discharge accumulates on the teats a few days before the big event. Milk may actually run from the teats during this time. The tissues around the head of the tail slacken, and the vaginal opening becomes larger and softer. Foaling is a private affair—mares like, if possible, to perform the miracle alone at night and, if watched, often seem able to hold their foal back until the human intruder has to go off for a bite to eat or a cup of tea.

The time taken in giving birth from the onset of the first visible contraction is normally between 30 and 60 minutes. As contractions intensify, the mare becomes restless and often shows signs as if she had colic. Do not interfere.

Once a foal is delivered, you can interfere only if the placental membranes are obstructing its nostrils (just tear a hole in them), but otherwise let the foal rest for a quarter of an hour. Never hurry separation of the umbilical cord linking dam and foal; it will break when one or the other eventually stands up.

The placenta, or afterbirth, follows the birth of the foal within one to three hours. It must all come away within 12 hours; otherwise veterinary advice is essential. If you find a rubbery brown "stone" in the afterbirth material, don't be alarmed. It is a hippomane—an agglomeration of cellular waste from the placental fluid. It is not significant but was once considered to be of enormous medical and magical value.

But suppose the mare is obviously in labor but no foal has been fully delivered within the normal space of one hour—what then? Call the veterinarian if two hours have passed from the time the first contractions were seen and the birth has not been completed. The veterinarian can correct problems of foaling manually, with drugs, or on rare occasions by cesarean section under general anesthetic. But I must emphasize that the vast majority of foalings come off without a hitch.

REARING

Foals are usually reared happily by their mothers without any need for human interference. Should difficulties arise, consult your veterinarian at once. There are, however, two points of general importance should the need to bottle-feed a foal arise:

1 The first milk (colostrum) produced by the mare in the 48 hours after foaling is essential for a healthy foal. Try to get some (even if it is only a teaspoonful) into the baby. If necessary, in emergencies, you can milk the mare. "Banks" of stored frozen colostrum do exist for special cases of need

CASTRATION

This process is also known as "gelding" or "cutting." Male ponies are castrated by surgical removal of their testicles harmlessly under an anesthetic if they are not required for breeding. The best age for the operation is when the animal is two years old, although it can be done as early as three months or much later in life if necessary. The operation does not take more than a few minutes to perform. The idea is to avoid unruly behavior as they get older, particularly when there are females in heat in the neighborhood, although some uncastrated males do live lives of utter decorum and have the most gentlemanly characters.

and you can be put in touch with one by your veterinarian if absolutely necessary.

2 Cow's milk is too rich for orphan foals and contains less sugar. To use cow's milk in an emergency, add three parts water (or, better, lime water—not lime cordial) to two parts milk and mix two teaspoonsful of brown sugar for each 1 pint (600 ml) of the mixture.

ACCIDENTS

Accidents will happen: collisions with fences, wire, glass, and the like, injuries in the field or on the road, mishaps in the stable or when one animal meets another. For most accidents you will usually need to consult the veterinarian, but you must have some idea of how to perform some simple first aid.

WOUNDS

These can be of all sizes, shapes, and severities from mere pinpricks to extensive lacerations. Whatever the cause or nature of the wound, there is a danger of infection developing. So, where the damage is more than very minor, it is wisest to call the veterinarian, who can protect the animal with injections or oral forms of antibacterial drugs.

First aid

This consists of stopping bleeding, which is achieved best by pressure from a pad of absorbent cotton, clean cloth, or even simply a clenched fist, and after cleaning the wound gently with warm water and a weak solution of an antiseptic, such as Betadine. However, if the wound is more than $1/2$ inch (1 cm) or so in length (and in the case of smaller wounds, those that are located on special areas such as eyelids), the veterinarian will probably need to put in a few nylon or other synthetic sutures. If there is a chance of this, don't mess up the

BELOW: *Cleaning a wound with antiseptic solution. Bleeding is controlled by applying firm pressure on a pad of absorbent cotton or gauze.*

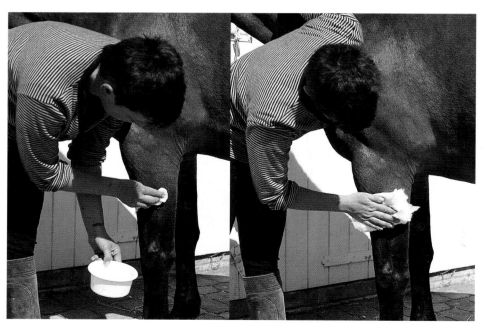

area with smelly antiseptic ointment after cleaning. If you feel the need to put something on, then call your veterinarian for advice.

If the wound is in a convenient place, such as a limb, then you can cover it with a light dressing, secured by bandaging.

There is always a risk of tetanus (lockjaw) in equines, particularly where wounds are deep, penetrating punctures that don't expose the damaged tissues to much air and that may be contaminated with dirt (see page 111). The tetanus bacterium thrives in airless wounds, particularly if there are chalky soil particles around. Tetanus can be introduced through the most insignificant-looking punctures that do not bleed or through nail pricks hidden under a shoe.

Consequently, all equines should always be protected against the disease by being vaccinated with the tetanus vaccine. The initial course is normally two injections at an interval of four to six weeks, with a booster shot a year later and then every three years or if an injury occurs.

BRUISES AND SPRAINS

You should tackle these injuries as soon as they happen in order to stop them from becoming established and turning slowly into other, more serious things. Both may present themselves as tender areas, possibly puffy and warm, and with resultant lameness if involving a limb. Your job is to stop the bleeding in the damaged area and to soothe the effects of the inflammation. Apply ice packs or cold water sponges, or hose the area with cold water for 20 or 30 minutes. Then either apply the special wet dressing, if possible, or bandage firmly. The bandage

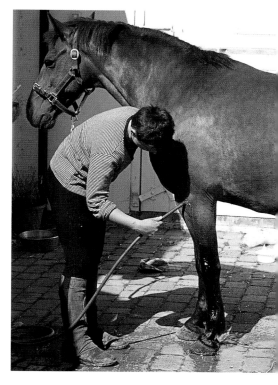

ABOVE: *Hosing down a sprain. Use cold water soon after it occurs, warm water if it has been there for longer than a few hours.*

restricts bleeding and fluid swelling of the tissues and gives support.

Note: Do not rub liniments on new injuries.

There is no reason why you shouldn't spray the affected area with a human-type pain-killing aerosol of the type used for burns, but note that lots of equines detest aerosols of any kind because they emit an irritating ultrasonic whine that is inaudible to humans but easily picked up by pony ears. Rest the animal. If the trouble persists for more than a day or two at the most, call the veterinarian.

SERIOUS ACCIDENTS

Should you be unlucky enough to have your pet involved in a serious accident, there are one or two basic things for you to do. If it is unable to rise or cannot walk, do not force it—send for the veterinarian and stay at the animal's head, talking quietly and stroking it to reassure it. Cover it with a blanket, sprinkled hay, or your jacket to keep it warm.

Don't try bottling anything into the animal, although if there is some water and sugar handy, see if it can drink a little voluntarily.

If there is major bleeding, control it with pressure at the point of hemorrhage by any means, including your knotted fist.

Don't fuss around with major injuries such as fractures; you may inflict more pain and shock. When the veterinarian arrives, he or she will have injections to relieve pain and quick-acting sedatives or injectable anesthesia if necessary.

FRACTURED LIMBS

These don't necessarily mean that the animal must be destroyed. Pet ponies aren't expected to win races like thoroughbreds and are much lighter built than their bigger relatives; racehorses need to have perfect legs and are unlikely to run exceptionally well after a break, while their size can make their healing a long, difficult process. Many fractures in equines can now be mended by internal fixation (special metal rods to hold broken bones together) and devices such as tough plastic casts, rather than plaster of Paris that isn't really strong enough to use on anything but foals and tiny ponies. Healing may take many months and the treatment is often expensive; your veterinarian will examine the animal and advise you, after determining the type and extent of the fracture, what is the kindest thing to do.

Lastly, don't panic. Keep calm—your pet depends on you to keep your head and think clearly.

EUTHANASIA

If an animal has to be euthanized, the veterinarian will do this task humanely, without fuss, and only for very good reasons. A merciful injection is instantaneous in its effect; you can ask your veterinarian to give a painless overdose of anesthetic intravenously. Discuss all alternatives with your veterinarian so you can make an informed decision that's right for you.

Enough of this gloom! It is more than likely that your pony will thrive and live on to a ripe old age without any unpleasant incidents. Wild ponies and asses don't live much beyond 20 or 25 years, with the occasional individual reaching the low thirties, but perhaps your pony will challenge the longevity record for a domesticated equine—no less than 61 years!

GLOSSARY

Bay
Red-brown color of the body with black mane, tail, and lower legs ("points").

Blaze
A broad white stripe running down the face.

Broken wind
Chronic lung damage causing heavy breathing and cough.

Brushing
The knocking of one leg by its opposite number when the pony is moving.

Cantle
The back of the saddle.

Cast
When a pony is unable to get up.

Cavesson
A noseband.

Chestnut
Reddish brown color of the body with similar or lighter mane and tail.

Clicking
The sound of one foot, usually the hind foot, coming into contact with the other. Clicking can cause damage and the pony may need boots or remedial shoeing.

Colic
A painful stomach/bowel condition.

Colt
An uncastrated male under three years of age.

Conformation
Term used to describe the shape and makeup of an animal.

Cow-hocked
The hock joints turn outward.

Crib biting
A "vice" in which a bored, stabled pony nibbles wood or other solid objects.

Dam
A pony's mother.

Dandy brush
A stiff brush used to remove dirt and mud from a pony's coat.

Dock
The top of the tail that contains the bony vertebrae.

Dorsal stripe
A dark stripe along a pony's back.

Dun
Brown, gold, or cream body color with darker mane, tail, and lower legs.

Fetlock
A projection behind and above the hoof.

Filly
A female under three years of age.

Forging
Hitting the underneath of the forefoot with the toe of the hind foot. This condition needs remedial shoeing.

Frog
The V-shaped pad on the sole of the hoof.

Gait
The leg movement of a pony.

Gelding
A castrated male.

Grazing muzzle
Muzzle used to restrict a pony's intake of grass in pasture.

Gray
A coat color produced by a mix of white and dark hairs.

Halter

A head harness, which is often made of rope, for leading the pony or tying it up.

Hand

A unit of measurement for ponies, equivalent to 4 inches (10 cm).

Head collar

A head harness comprising a noseband, headpiece, and throat lash, which is used for leading or tying up a pony.

Hock

The joint at the tarsus (ankle).

Jibbing

A refusal to go forward.

Laminitis

A painful disease caused by the inflammation of tissues within the hoof. It can be recurrent.

Livery

Rent-paid accommodation, sometimes with daily care included.

Manger

A feed trough.

New Zealand rug

A tough waterproof blanket for continuous use outdoors.

Near side

The pony's left side.

Numnah

A wool or cotton pad used under the saddle to relieve pressure and absorb sweat.

Off side

The pony's right side.

Palomino

A bright chestnut or gold body color with a white mane and tail. In the United States, a recognized breed.

Pastern

The part of the foot between the fetlock and the hoof.

Piebald

Black and white patches on the coat.

Pommel

The raised front of a saddle.

Roller

A broad strap around the belly to keep a blanket in position.

Rig

A male with one undescended testicle.

Roan

A mixture of white and other colored hairs evenly distributed over the body.

Roaring

A loud noise made by a galloping pony due to faults in the vocal chords.

Sandcrack

A vertical split in the hoof wall.

Seedy toe

Bad-smelling rot of the hoof wall.

Skewbald

Brown and white patches on the coat.

Snaffle

The most common type of bit, usually with one ring on each side.

Snip

A small white mark on the nose.

Sock

White pastern and fetlock.

Sound

Healthy in all respects.

Speedy cut

A wound to one leg caused by contact with another when the pony is moving fast.

Stable blanket

A blanket used in the stable.

Stallion

An uncastrated male that is over three years of age.

Staring coat

A dull coat, often with the hairs standing up.

Star

A white patch on the forehead.

Surcingle

A strap going around the belly to fix a blanket in place.

Strawberry

A pink-looking roan color composed of a mix of chestnut and white hairs.

Tack

The equipment worn by a pony, including the saddle and bridle, etc.

Tendon

A gristly band of tissue that attaches a muscle to a bone.

Tetanus

A serious disease caused by a micro-organism that enters the body, typically through a wound.

Vice

A bad habit. Stable vices occur in ponies that are kept in stables for long periods of time. Boredom can lead to such vices as crib biting, weaving, and wind sucking.

Walleyed

Blue or blue and white eyes.

Weaving

A "vice" in which a bored, stabled pony rocks its head and neck from side to side stereotypically.

Windgall

A puffy fluid-filled swelling above the fetlock that does not cause lameness.

Withers

The high point of the back, located at the base of the neck between the animal's shoulder blades.

USEFUL ADDRESSES

American Connemara Pony Society
32600 Fairmount Blvd.
Pepper Pike, OH 44124
www.nas.com/acps

American Miniature Horse Association
5601 South Interstate 35 W
Alvarado, TX 76009
information@amha.org

American Shetland Pony Club
81B Queenwood Rd.
Morton, IL 61550
info@shetlandminiature.com

American Walking Pony Association
PO Box 5282
Macon, GA 31211

American Welara Pony Society
PO Box 401
Yucca Valley, CA 92284
awps@eu.e-universe.com

Dartmoor Pony Society of America
145 Upper Ridge View Rd.
Columbus, NC 28722
deuterpony@aol.com

Pony of the Americas Club, Inc.
5240 Elmwood Ave.
Indianapolis, IN 46203
poac@poac.org

United States Pony Clubs, Inc.
4041 Iron Works Parkway
Lexington, KY 40511
www.ponyclub.org

ACKNOWLEDGMENTS

The publishers would like to thank the following people for their help in compiling this book:

Linzi Aiken BHSAI

Claire Baker BHSPI

Melanie Faldo

Anita French of Culford Stables, Bury St Edmunds

Peter Hay of Bridlepath Saddlery, St John's Street, Bury St Edmunds, Suffolk IP33 1SN (Tel: 01284 754124)

INDEX

INDEX